Praise for *The Promise of Language*

"A hip collage that overlays the New York streets, the classroom, the library, and the record store—and is enlivened by radical politics and brushes with celebrities—Gilyard's tart autobiographical Künstlerroman brilliantly modernizes the chronicle of Black writers who came of age during the Civil Rights era and went on to create the Black Arts Movement."
—Lawrence Jackson, Johns Hopkins University

"In *The Promise of Language*, poet, scholar, and essayist Keith Gilyard has dropped a major and critical contribution into the canon of African American experience, language, art, and culture. With honest and poetic storytelling, each page has a breathtaking urgency to the complex, dangerous, and beautiful growing up of a Black boy in the era of Civil Rights, Black Power, and the Black Arts Movement. If he were a painter, the first glance would take your breath away. If this were music, it'd be listened to over and over. It is all of that and poetic prose, written as honest and compelling as the blues, as emotional as soul, and as innovative and complex as jazz."
—Michael Simanga, author of *Amiri Baraka and the Congress of African People*

THE PROMISE
OF LANGUAGE

African American Life Series

A complete listing of the books in this series can
be found online at wsupress.wayne.edu.

SERIES EDITOR

Melba Joyce Boyd
Department of Africana Studies, Wayne State University

THE PROMISE OF LANGUAGE

A Memoir

Keith Gilyard

WAYNE STATE UNIVERSITY PRESS
DETROIT

© 2025 by Keith Gilyard. All rights reserved. No part of this book may be reproduced without formal permission.

ISBN 9780814351949 (paperback)
ISBN 9780814351956 (ebook)

Library of Congress Control Number: 2024939540

Cover design by Nathaniel Roy.

Grateful acknowledgment is made to the Arthur L. Johnson African American Studies Endowment Fund and the Thelma Gray James Fund for the generous support of the publication of this volume.

Wayne State University Press rests on Waawiyaataanong, also referred to as Detroit, the ancestral and contemporary homeland of the Three Fires Confederacy. These sovereign lands were granted by the Ojibwe, Odawa, Potawatomi, and Wyandot Nations, in 1807, through the Treaty of Detroit. Wayne State University Press affirms Indigenous sovereignty and honors all tribes with a connection to Detroit. With our Native neighbors, the press works to advance educational equity and promote a better future for the earth and all people.

Wayne State University Press
Leonard N. Simons Building
4809 Woodward Avenue
Detroit, Michigan 48201-1309

Visit us online at wsupress.wayne.edu.

For Mary Lewis Gilyard

Author's Note

The *Promise of Language* has a different purpose than my previous memoir writing, most notably *Voices of the Self: A Study of Language Competence* (1991). In that book, I created a narrative that served as a data set for analysis as I intervened in conversations about relationships between formal schooling and speakers of African American Language. Then, drawing on the fields of education, linguistics, psychology, and sociology, I performed the analysis. Decades later, I shift rhetorical gears. The focus in this present book is on my evolution as a writer who has produced not only scholarship but poetry, fiction, and popular essays. The storytelling angle has shifted. Virtually all the dialogue and scholarly apparatus are gone. What remains is the central drama: my emergence through family, community, and school experiences against the backdrop of the Cold War and of the civil rights, Black Power, and Black Arts movements. This book is a prequel to all that I have accomplished in academe and is a contribution in the tradition of African American letters on how language shapes lives and how lives shape language.

Acknowledgments

I thank all who have mentored and inspired me along the way. Although that's too lengthy a list to include in this space, I hope folks feel the vibes. I also give a special shout-out to the five people who were most insistent that I produce this story: Adam Banks, Earl Brooks, Arthur Flowers, Mudiwa Pettus, and Geneva Smitherman.

I

Like most children, I was a sucker for crafted language. Rhythmic, flowing, metaphorical. The only question being which languages would satisfy the craving. Harlem street words for one. Before I reached waist-high to my mother or father, I had been saturated with that *What you mean, jellybean?* That *What I said, cabbage head. I bet you a fat man. What you got cookin, good lookin? What's your story, morning glory? If I say a mosquito can pull a plow, hitch that muthafucka up! See you later, alligator. After a while, crocodile. Must be jelly.* All that neo-countrified slickness just in the mix tuned my ears early. Then, right on time, I got hit with Jocko Henderson.

See, like many baby boomers, I arrived in the middle of a paradigm shift in the media. Television was booming. At the end of World War II, only a few thousand television sets were in American homes. By my debut early in 1952, the same time NBC launched *The Today Show* and CBS rolled out *The Guiding Light*, the number approached 15 million. Ratings and advertising money were being transferred to the new, spellbinding medium, and as a result radio was in decline. In 1953 Dinah Washington sang "TV Is the Thing This Year." Undoubtedly she sang the literal truth on her hit record, although we know that Dinah took it elsewhere when she purred about the television repairman adjusting her dials channel by channel. She finally burst out, kind of spoiling the metaphor, that when they hit Channel 11 she cried out to her mama about how good the repairman was treating her mama's daughter. But my understanding all that is running a little ahead of the story. The main point for now is that Dinah gave voice to the new media reality. To save the day for the older entertainment entity, radio executives countered with Black appeal radio. Stations targeted young African Americans with rhythm and blues records and showed that niche programs were commercially viable. The broadcasts bailed out a failing industry and served as the precursor to the Top 40 format. Ironically, the radio people had Dinah Washington on *their* side.

2

That's where Jocko Henderson came in. A disc jockey of the new Black appeal, he emerged in and from Philadelphia to feature on his *Rocket Ship Show* not just the hits but some of the quickest and hippest lingo in the Northeast: *eee-tiddlee-yock / this is the Jock / I'm back on the scene / with the record machine / saying ooh, poppa day / I'm on my way.* Just thrilling to me. Incredible and indelible. I got the rap alternating with the music. Clyde McPhatter escaping from the Dominoes. Fats Domino, thrill on blueberry hill. Ruth Brown, oh, what a dream. The Champs had my main jam, "Tequila." They weren't a Black band, but they rode that mambo beat and Danny Flores's saxophone to a number one hit. I dug the energy of that saxophone. Around the same time, the Coasters hit with "Yakety Yak," rhyming playfully and featuring King Curtis on saxophone riffing so melodically. All that orchestrated by Jocko.

So those were two of the broad expressive strokes—streets and radio—whose appealing sounds punctuated my youth. And Jocko eventually made it to television as well. The specifics of how and why my parents endorsed these passions for me, at least the media part, since they mostly controlled what I received through the airwaves, are beyond the veil of recall. But they were still youthful, for sure. My mother had been an attractive, bosomy, coffee-colored party girl down in Ocilla, Georgia, hanging out with her uncle, Fred Jackson, who was a dapper fellow known as the Maestro. They would go on weekend trips to clubs—juke joints, I guess—down in Tallahassee, Florida. That was about one hundred miles away. This was during the time my father was away in the army. They weren't married yet. My mother said she would be there when he got out. She didn't say anything about sitting around on her hands until he returned. I recall that one of her favorite sayings was "You better straighten up and fly right"—usually issued as a warning to me that I was flying wrong. Nowadays I know that this is the title of a popular Nat King Cole tune that came out in 1944, when my mother was seventeen. And in the late 1950s she was a huge fan of Jackie Wilson and Sam Cooke. That preference never ended. Only David Ruffin and Marvin Gaye could come along and hang with them later. Black appeal radio had her pegged right. My father went more for swing bands: Jimmie Lunceford, Count Basie. I think he had some exposure in the military. But he knew that Dinah Washington recording. When I brought up her name decades later, he said, "TV Is the Thing This Year."

3

Church rhythms claimed their due as well. Seems like destiny. I was born on a Sunday afternoon in the old Lutheran Hospital of Manhattan on 144th Street, across a narrow street from Convent Avenue Baptist Church. You can still see the hospital's name etched into the building. I heard that someone, besides offering a cigar, told my father to get me across the street as soon as possible because he had a feeling about me, whatever that meant.

Those climbs up the steep incline to the church after exiting Colonial Park at Edgecombe Avenue seriously taxed my unsteady legs in the early years. I remember leaning into cold, harsh winds to make it. But the majesty of the arrival validated the trek, as I was continually struck anew by the huge gray cinder blocks that comprised the façade. The stained windows and the gigantic organ pipes, the largest in Harlem, accented the sanctuary. This is where Martin Luther King Jr. made his last New York appearance, a week before his assassination in Memphis.

I don't know who was responsible for us attending that church. Maybe it was one of the few things on which my parents agreed. They were both involved—she in the day nursery, he as a deacon—before any memories I have of the church. In the February 9, 1957, edition of the *New York Age Defender*, in the "Worship in New York" section, an article about the church's upcoming anniversary celebration appears. I was four years old, almost five. Above the article is a photograph of officers and members of the trustees and deacon boards. Thirty-six men surround the legendary pastor, Dr. John W. Saunders, who is front and center. Of those, I remember Lorenzo Pierson, an energetic and engaging man, in my mind a leader among deacons. He was vocal on bus outings and at softball games. My father is not in the photo. His name, Hezekiah Gilyard, is the last one mentioned in the caption among those of the members not present. I joked with him about this one time. *Pops, this some kind of omen. Your name there but you absent.* He didn't think that humorous.

At any rate, Pastor Saunders had put together a powerful institution, with a teeming membership, by the time he suffered a stroke in 1955. He was almost ninety years old then. I knew his name, but the active leadership baton had gone to Reverend Mannie I. Wilson, another dynamo, although I remember mostly sitting through the sermons of Reverend Fredrick Bailey. I sometimes spotted my father stationed in the front row or walking the aisles to serve Communion. I liked Bailey's cadences and the stories. I obviously listened to more Bible than I could read. I wasn't fearing the Lord that much. I figured that, had He wanted to, he would have gotten me for sneaking money from the collection plate to buy candy. A boy in church taught me to put in money and, supposedly taking change, take out more than I'd put in. Having to account for it in my mind, I rationalized that He had everything and didn't need the cash. Neither did I need the candy. But I'd work all that philosophy out later. My sister Barbara wouldn't do what I did. I think she was more into the gospel, although no more into the gospel music than I was. Howard Ruthus Mann, the minister of music, had the singers on point. If I had that soul Reverend Bailey talked about, they were touching it. With all the language flow of those live performances, the pageantry, the swooning women who caught the spirit, the lessons of Sunday school—*for God so loved the world*—and my sister's urging, I presented myself for baptism at the age of eight, one minute after she did. She was nine. The glory of it all could not be resisted. Wash all my sins away.

However, the road to the baptismal pool wasn't quite that straightforward. Twists and turns always were in play and reflected, of course, in language—again the problem of which language was going to be important in my life. Certainly, I heard more from the streets. I trailed my mother to the beauty parlor some Saturdays and became fascinated by tales of some sorry-ass dude who wasn't ever gon git right. Or maybe stories about a dude who indeed proved right. Television repairman right. *Ooh, chile.* Could be the same dude! Just don't get caught looking too interested. *Stop lookin in my mouth, boy!* I had to chill like Claudia and Frieda, those little MacTeer girls in Toni Morrison's *The Bluest Eye.* Be shackled on the edge of the language but getting enough of the drift.

The shackles came off when I started school at PS 90 on 148th Street. Kindergarten was held for only half a day back then, and it became freedom time at high noon. I had three and a half blocks to walk home through what to me was an urban wonderland. The journey took a couple of hours every day. I ran wild along 8th Avenue with some of the fellas. Peeped into bars and barbershops, though I was leery at first about barbershops because Albert Anastasia, a Mafioso, got blasted in one and I'd seen pictures in the newspaper. We threw stones at winos asleep in doorways. Followed the horse-drawn vegetable wagon. Get the work in.

Don't worry about the mule going blind. Or we headed north a few blocks up 8th Avenue toward the Polo Grounds, where the New York Giants, my father's favorite team, played their last game the month I started school. I didn't know anything about baseball, at least nothing I remember from that far back, although my father had taken me to a game or two. People in places along 8th Avenue did know a lot about the sport and appreciated departing star Willie Mays. He hit thirty-five home runs and stole thirty-eight bases that season, his second 30-30 campaign in a row. Or we'd race across 148th Street, being careful about the traffic, headed for Colonial Park, what they now call Jackie Robinson Park. Sometimes an older person would ask what we "little midget muthafuckas" were up to. We'd always say "Nothing." We'd fight. Climb the hill. Throw rocks. Wrestle. Tear our pants. Try to ruin the shoes on which our parents spent hard-earned money. Get our jackets dirty. Or maybe we would venture east and get glimpses of 7th Avenue, maybe even another block east to Lenox Avenue.

Naturally, my mother had to put a stop to this. Usually a worker outside the home, a hatmaker by trade, she stayed home those days because she had become pregnant with her fourth and last child around the time I started school. I swore I always came straight home, a story that simply didn't add up. It was what my mother termed a cold-ass argument, pretty much meaning the opposite of what the phrase means today. That's how language can flip. There was a time when athletes who were considered bums were called dogs or were accused of dogging it. Now, calling an athlete a dog is about the highest compliment you can pay. Anyway, after several warnings, my mother grabbed a belt and touched me up to get me back in line, curtailing the exploits and some of the storytelling. As she grew more and more pregnant and less energetic, I would pick my spots to test her. I couldn't let her shut me all the way down. People say I was hardheaded that way—or what some old folks called a willful child.

We kids had no real concept of the peril. Harlem was in reality a sprawling ghetto. You can tell it wasn't planned to be that way because it possessed some of the widest avenues and once had some of the most artful and solid housing stock in Manhattan. In fact, it had been a White neighborhood at the turn of the century before Blacks started moving uptown, accelerated by the construction of Penn Station, which displaced many. Later came the move to escape deteriorating conditions in

6

the middle West Side, the areas once known as the Tenderloin and San Juan Hill. Speculators in Harlem had guessed wrong and overbuilt, leaving vacancies they were happy to overcharge Blacks to fill. Harlem had turned nearly all Black by 1930, and waves of migration continued from other parts of Manhattan, the South (my parents), the Caribbean, and Africa. But Harlem soon declined comprehensively. Recovery from the Great Depression was minimal. Black frustration fueled the riots of 1935 and 1943. The prime downtown-to-uptown White party nights of the Harlem Renaissance had long disappeared, and Black elites were moving away. Landlords began subdividing units to maximize profits. They neglected tenement buildings that subsequently fell into severe disrepair. Roaches and rats multiplied endlessly. We had a large trap under the kitchen sink that didn't save our pet turtles. The ruthless invaders who evaded the trap ate out their stomachs. We didn't see any point in replacing the turtles. I learned that you should clean a baby thoroughly before putting her to sleep. If traces of milk were on her or her clothes, she could get attacked.

My parents might have felt that in choosing Harlem they had fallen for the okey-doke. My fellow Harlem native James Baldwin, who was around the age of my parents, had described things aptly in "The Harlem Ghetto." He wrote, "All over Harlem, Negro boys and girls are growing into stunted maturity, trying desperately to find a place to stand; and the wonder is not that so many are ruined but that so many survive." I didn't have the perspective to think in terms of personal ruin. As folks say, it was what it was.

Everybody locked themselves into their apartments resolutely. We had two or three locks on the door, including the bar that wedged against the door and fit into a slot in the floor. Heroin had become plentiful, and junkies abounded. Seems they sprang up like cicadas, nodding and scratching and outnumbering the winos. That's really a low-energy hangout most days. I couldn't fathom why a person would choose such a life. When I first heard about junkies, I thought they were a unique breed with some weird and special distinguishing characteristics. Like sci-fi aliens. I needed to see some. Then one day this ruckus occurred outside our apartment. We were on the top floor, the sixth, in the unit closest to the staircase. Cops were chasing two men who were headed to the roof. I was in the doorway peeping from behind my mother when the men, who a neighbor referred to as junkies, were brought down, handcuffed and buck naked. Nothing strange about them except their being naked.

One reason I was captivated during my high school years by Claude Brown's classic *Manchild in the Promised Land*, despite some of its untenable plotting and overwrought fantasy concerning the crime and violence he participated in, is that Brown described exactly the promised land where we both once lived. He resided on 8th Avenue at 146th Street during the early 1950s. I was right around the corner on 146th Street, on the short block between 8th Avenue and Bradhurst Avenue, right across the street from the pool in Colonial Park, the park separating us from the money people up on Sugar Hill. At least fifteen times in the book he mentioned 146th Street or Colonial Park or PS 90, which he attended. I had read no other literature focused on where I had lived and represented the lens through which I remember first looking out at the world. I imagined a teenage Claude—or Sonny, as he was known—winking at me as he passed my stroller, saying, "Yeah, little man, it's rough out here."

2

My memory of the environment surrounding school is clearer than my memory of school itself. Not that I lacked eagerness. In some ways the competitive second child, I couldn't wait to get up in there with my sister. I had been tracking her progress, constantly nosy about any material she brought home. As I always say, she served as my first reading teacher, backed up by my mother, who kept us both going. Barbara kept the lead; she remained smarter than me all through our school years. But I could stay close.

For a research project, I interviewed my mother about the beginning of my education. She said I took to school, to quote her, like a duck to water. Barbara had the emotional issue of leaving home, crying and carrying on. On the other hand, I was fine. My mother recalled it exactly the way I did. Beyond that, she conveyed that her expectations were high for me because she saw no reason I shouldn't succeed. However, she didn't mention all the hours she spent going over lessons with me. In fact, it was while performing for my mother that I received my lifelong reading scar. She was seated in a chair as I stood in front of her, reading from a primer. Why this made my sister Pat, three years old, come up from behind and slice the left side of my face with a razor blade we'll never know. Wasn't literacy complicated enough? What was her framework? I don't remember any pain, just blood and pandemonium, all the yelling and screaming and swirl of motion. My mother decided not to have my wound stitched. Medical folks weren't as good in the 1950s as they are now, and she feared I would be left with railroad tracks. So my "distinguishing mark" healed on its own—for the better, I think. And it's funny about Pat. She has been my partner forever in all manner of adventures—except for that one.

Past that obstacle, I negotiated school matters as my mother expected, though I'm not sure she understood what an important model she was. She read all the time, always did word puzzles, always tried to occupy us with written material. She could be prescriptive about grammar, getting on your nerves sometimes. One day I was looking at the flavors listed on the buttons of a soda machine. I announced that I wanted to try burgundy, but I pronounced it bur GUN dy. "Bur GUN dy?" my mother chided. "Now how that sound?" I knew I had pronounced the word incorrectly. However, not liking the reproach, I responded, "Yeah, how *does* that sound?" She replied, "Oh, now you smart," as she lightly cuffed me upside the head. Then she bought me that soda.

If, as a young Ebonics speaker and gospel-inflected and sermon-inflected Jocko lover in Harlem, I learned the standardized prescriptions and the juggling of language varieties early, my mother was the major reason. At least that's what the sociolinguists tell me. They contend that women generally fluctuate more than men in terms of language modes and use a greater concentration of prestigious forms. Indeed, my mother seemed to be a language chameleon. I had witnessed her speak different ways to family, neighbors, grocers, salespeople, doctors, church people, and school officials. Although she was born and raised in Georgia, she never, over all the years, sounded Black southern to me. But then she had been in New York City since the 1940s. She was Black enough, certainly Black enough in the beauty parlor, but not so southern in accent as her sisters and brothers or my grandmother. Not so Black and southern as my grandmother's second husband.

I have wondered how my biological grandfather fit in language wise. A successful businessman, he died when my mother was just shy of nine years old, and I never heard her speak of him with anything but reverence. I think she, his eldest daughter, was a daddy's girl. But I wonder how much she was a daddy imitator linguistically. Did he display some of the versatility I heard from her? Several times while in Ocilla I listened to elders tell me about my grandfather, Charles Otis Lewis, and recall his wit and prominent civic reputation. It never occurred to me to ask how he sounded, the style and timbre of his verbal game. My mother did tell me about an incident in church when my grandfather dozed off and was needled by the pastor to pay attention. My grandfather calmly adjusted his hat brim and replied casually that when he heard something worth paying attention to he would. That sounds like my mother talking. Sounds like me sometimes. My grandfather succumbed to illness in January 1936. He had a brand-new automobile that he didn't get a chance to drive.

10

His daughter graduated from the Ocilla public school system in 1946. That's another language factor I wonder about: the influence of teachers. Who taught the grammar rules and pushed the civics lessons? According to my mother, her class was the first Black senior class in Ocilla's history in which every eligible student registered to vote. They stood all day in the rain to achieve the feat. I used to think no Black people registered to vote in Georgia back then. But that wasn't true in Irwin County, which happens to be the county where Jefferson Davis was captured. The poll tax had been repealed; the White primary had been struck down by the courts. My mother and her classmates acted before the blistering White-supremacist countermeasures prevailed. My mother never missed a chance to exercise the franchise. Election Day was the one day you knew she would arrive home late from work because she had to stop by the voting booth. I came to find out that she was an FDR baby, always spoke well of the man who was president from the time she was six until she was eighteen. Little surprise that she became a confirmed Democrat. She liked Kennedy, Carter, and the Clintons. Chose Hillary Clinton over Barack Obama in the primary, arguing that a woman should get a chance. Stubborn as she is, she would never admit to voting for Obama in the general election, but I know she did.

So that shows a bit more of the Mary Lewis Gilyard mindset and skill set with which I grew up. Language examples abounded, but she made sure she was the lead pattern. The sociolinguists also say that, despite the angst of many parents, the greatest language influence on you once you reach adolescence is your peer group. I once accepted that claim at face value. I now agree only if we are talking about the ability of a peer group to get you to speak a particular way on particular occasions. Speaking that one way is not necessarily all that you perform. Your tribe could be trickster figures, and you could have been groomed for membership by your mother. You were not always going to risk your health and give a snide answer to the essential query: "Now how that sound?" Nevertheless, you were developing the approach she favored. Some sociolinguists claim that kind of discernment shows up later in adolescence. That is way late. Rudolph Troike, for example, in a piece titled "Receptive Bidialectalism," argued that the youngest schoolchildren have learned much about language and social differences and can match utterances to social contexts. I have no reason to disagree. When I started school, my receptive bidialectalism was in full effect and the productive side, the biloquialism, was coming along. You never merely reproduce language for long. You're a little scientist, a trickster scientist, experimenting with combinations, working every single day trying to get language to work for you.

One aspect is deriving pleasure from print. You'll read your ass off if that dynamic is in play. Stories are therefore essential, and reading is the most efficient way for most of us to expand conception. Stories are the first passport to what's happening in the wider world or at least to see what fantasies and fun are out there. As the educator John Rouse wrote in *The Completed Gesture*, "Life will never be a substitute for literature, it's not long enough."

I remember *Curious George* was a favorite of mine. That monkey George got into all kinds of trouble while trying to avoid being locked up in the zoo. I didn't want him locked up. *Just keep on getting into trouble, George.* Academics later talked about George as a colonial subject, tricked and captured in Africa by the Man in the Yellow Hat and subjected to a Middle Passage and enslavement in America. There do be some politics in them kiddie books for real. But I was decades away from that understanding about George. I didn't see the monkey as a symbol for Africans and didn't know anything about slavery. I just wanted George to win. What's fascinating to me now is that the creators, Margaret Rey and H. A. Rey, could not envision George prevailing even though they themselves had escaped from the Nazis. They avoided fascism, but George went to the zoo.

I did know that *The Amos 'n' Andy Show* and some cartoons were stereotypical or even racist, although I didn't have the vocabulary to describe them that way. My mother thought Kingfish especially silly and irksome, nothing like her father. I could see some humor in Andy but didn't follow the trail of reruns into the 1960s as many others did.

I don't recall any great emotional response to Dick and Jane, with baby sister Sally and dog Spot and cat Puff. Those were the best-selling readers in the 1950s. We had them and had to get through this introduction to a version of White America. That was some politics as well. I didn't know Dr. Seuss hated the Dick and Jane books, taking dead aim at them with works like *The Cat in the Hat*, which dropped the year I started school and was a big hit with me. Seuss's zany rhyming scored much higher on the scale of playful imagination than Dick and Jane. Those Dr. Seuss racial and ethnic stereotypes that became big news in fall 2021? That's discussion for another day.

All told, my mother didn't worry about school. Her attitude was that I should simply do well, which I apparently did, according to the written record. My teachers judged me satisfactory in reading and oral communication. They said I possessed confidence, took initiative, got along well with other kids, was moderately aggressive, and occasionally resented group control. Supposedly, I didn't require a lot of attention and could focus on work for sustained periods. I don't recall enough to judge their assessments in detail, but all that strikes me as being right.

Back then students were tracked into so-called ability groups. In first grade I was tracked into what was considered the highest group. That may or may not have been beneficial for me. The key point for these purposes, though, is that the outcome was not unlikely, given my experiences. I surely had no linguistic deprivation to overcome. However, school still loomed as a problem if one stepped back and took the broad view. Twenty-five percent of the elementary school students in the New York City public system were African American, and we were highly concentrated in a de facto segregated institution. Psychologist Kenneth Clark, who had impact on the *Brown* decision, declared that the ruling should apply to places like Harlem. We might start out okay in PS 90, but numbers suggested that, as a group, the longer we stayed in that school the worse we would perform. The Black units in the system lagged on all achievement tests.

A considerable body of literature suggests that the third grade was key. Black students began to fall behind after that point. That never could have been about potential. Children perceive more at nine years old than they do at five. They know more about what a Harlem is and is not. They know more about social disparity and how to read White attitudes, especially those of backward teachers and political figures. Even if only intuitively, they know, after four years filtered through these Black ghettoes and Black educational units, that the prevailing voice of White America is saying fuck you louder and louder as they grow older. By the end of third grade, they're old enough to say fuck you, too.

My mother wouldn't allow things to go that far. By the end of 1958, we would leave Harlem for Corona, Queens. Some people uptown called it Long Island, which used to confuse me until I discovered what they meant. Although Queens is legally one of the five boroughs of New York City, it sits—along with Brooklyn, Nassau County, and Suffolk County—on the 118-mile-long land mass known as Long Island. It is Queens and Long Island at the same time. Whatever the name, my parents, through the GI Bill, bought a two-family house on tree-lined 34th Avenue, just east of Jackson Heights, which itself was a segregated formation designed to accommodate White population spillover from overcrowded Manhattan once enough transportation arteries were in place. We would be a block beyond Junction Boulevard, which should have been named Division Boulevard because of its function as a racial boundary. Later it would be called a northern Mason-Dixon Line. But no economic stigma was attached, at least not initially. Some of the homes on our side of the line were better than those, mainly apartments, on the other side. We would not be in the ghetto.

The transition is blurry to me. Of course, I always assume my mother was the driving force because I see her as the striver. Preferring to try New York City, she had turned down an offer of land to remain in Georgia, an offer made by my father's relatively prosperous stepfather. But a run-down tenement in Harlem in no way matched her idea of progress, especially not with four kids. My father had to agree, I suppose. I equivocate because I don't have a strong sense of his presence or voice during those early years. In retrospect, I'm guessing that he would have preferred to remain in Georgia and become a landowner. I know he, whose nickname was Muletrain, had vowed never to walk behind his stepfather's mule again, but I think he was favorably disposed, especially given that he hadn't advanced beyond primary school, to working his own land. He would have accepted that sequel to the military, where, as he expressed it, "them crackers was something else," especially at and around Camp McCain in Grenada County, Mississippi.

Indeed, Whites flashed extreme hostility toward African American soldiers in Starkville, Grenada, and the village of Duck Hill, the latter located only a quarter mile from camp. On July 3, 1943, four soldiers of Company L, 470th Quartermaster Truck Regiment, holding overnight passes, traveled to Starkville, eighty miles away. As they were trying to return to camp, two White policemen accosted them on the street and beat them with nightsticks. The soldiers were jailed and beaten again, then released the next morning to a military detachment for the journey back to Camp McCain. As word of the incident spread around the company, a group of soldiers wanted to procure a truck to drive to Starkville to "teach a lesson," but one of the victims, Sergeant Harry Jones, apparently persuaded the men otherwise. Still simmering that night, a group of about twenty soldiers from Company L, fully armed because they had been on the rifle range that day and still had their weapons for cleaning, marched to the railroad tracks outside Duck Hill and riddled several buildings with bullets, terrifying the residents inside. However, no one was injured in the assault. My father, twenty years old at the time, was confined to the camp that night because of KP duty but heard the gunfire, as did superior officers. Six men were court-martialed, convicted, and received prison sentences of ten to fifteen years.

I mostly remember my father being in church, though it seems he showed up in the building but didn't walk there with us. I remember a time when my family was ill. Everybody except me was laid up with bad colds, or maybe it was the flu. My parents called me into their bedroom and, lying in bed, told me that I had to go to the grocery store on 8th Avenue. What is clear to me about my father is that he was a big athletic man who I figured could do anything involving strength and mobility. This was the only time I saw him needing help. He gave me a piece of paper identifying the desired items and folded that around some bills. My mother reminded me to come straight back home. It's the only joint instruction from them, the only joint image, really, that I recall. I don't even have pictures, not one.

Incidentally, pertaining to visuals, I think of "Harlem 1958," Art Kane's famous photograph of jazz musicians gathered on 126th Street. I had heard of Count Basie but not of Dizzy Gillespie, Roy Eldridge, Mary Lou Williams, Sonny Rollins, Thelonious Monk, Benny Golson, Art Blakey, Marian McPartland, Charles Mingus, Horace Silver, Lester Young, or the other forty-five musicians in the shot. Probably unlike most, I focus on the twelve boys seated on the curb alongside Basie. I would have fit in seamlessly.

My father was the last person, coming from a farm and then the military, who should have tried living in New York. He married my mother in 1946 and found himself in Claude Brown country surrounded by more glitter around the island of Manhattan than he could have envisioned.

He thought he could obtain some for himself through gambling, which was the wrong call for the country boy. Not to mention the women. My father told me that he never chased them. That's only because, with his tall, reddish-brown magnetism, he didn't have to.

It's weird, or maybe not so weird if I go archival hard enough, but I have a clear image of Ike sitting in our living room up in Harlem talking with us. He wore a beret and used to call me Lil Rock. I didn't know he was Ike "Rock" Williams, the great boxer who had been world lightweight champion for six years and was also notable for having been managed by the mobster Blinky Palermo. Williams had been retired for a couple of years when I met him at our apartment. But the grown-ups never told us much. I'm guessing that my Aunt Georgia was involved. She knew Johnny Saxton, who had been a stablemate of Williams. It's too much to nail down. Always a mystery to Barbara and me. Sometimes, speaking of the early days, we'll still ask each other, "Remember Ike?" I will never assemble a completely coherent narrative, one accounting for all the connections, frustrations, conflicts, and sensitivities. I don't even have that desire anymore. Auntie told me once, when I was on a trip with her to Massachusetts, that my father was alright and that I should never be too hard on him because nothing is ever one way. She said she knew her sister, the person who, even as ultimately loyal as she proved to be, could see a fire break out in our kitchen behind the refrigerator, snatch up me and one-year-old Barbara, and rush from the apartment without alerting her husband. Luckily, my father stirred in time to avoid catastrophe. I'm not sure why Mary could do things like that, but she could.

Speaking of Auntie, my first babysitter, she is the sole person responsible for keeping one of my locutions alive. I can't even remember when she asked me if I knew my name. I was two or three years old. I gave her the epic version: "I'm Keith the Gilyard." Like I was Erik the Red, William the Conqueror, or Attila the Hun. I have no idea why I announced that. Anyway, she thought it was the funniest thing and often, in her mid-nineties, still refers to me that way. I'll answer the phone, "Hi, Auntie." She'll respond, "Hey, the Gilyard."

Despite apparent delusions of grandeur, I began to stutter in those early years. Fortunately, it didn't last long. My sisters seized on it and teased me, talking over me before I could get my words out. That was the greatest offense. *My words!* I had to get it together to combat losses at home and in the street. If a group from neighboring PS 89 encountered students from my school, they were quick to shout, "PS 90, kiss our hiney." That used to burn me up. They always had the initiative. We would try to rhyme a good comeback. You can imagine some obvious ones. But we never seemed to get even.

3

Ears have their own categories. "Volare." I always liked that song. Nah, nobody was flying but Superman. I didn't even know what the Italian words meant. Just loved the sound of the language. It was a big hit for Domenico Modugno as we arrived in Corona intact: Moms, Pops, Barbara, Pat, infant Frances, and me. The Irish and Italians were on the run. What looked better to my parents looked worse to them. This sort of transition was occurring in enclaves all over Queens. It's the history of the borough—neighborhood change after neighborhood change, with Queens eventually becoming the most ethnically diverse county in the United States.

We were located halfway between PS 92, on our side of Junction Boulevard, and PS 149, which was a block on the other side in largely Jewish Jackson Heights. We went to check out 92 first. For a long time I thought we were turned away on grounds of overcrowding and directed instead to PS 149. But my mother later said she had a choice and picked 149 because she thought it the better school. It looked decidedly more modern than PS 92, which was built in 1906, whereas 149 was a Public Works Administration project, only about twenty years old. Barbara and I were registered and then escorted to class by the principal, Mr. Price, whose pants were too long and repeatedly got caught under the heels of his shoes. I was placed in low-level 1-4, although I had been in high-level 1-1 in Harlem. That's how they started their program with me. How I started with them was to stick to the formality of "Raymond," my given first name, which I used only in school. I was shocked to see so many White kids in one room. That had never happened before. Predominately White students and predominately Jews. (I understood Jews to be White.) They wouldn't know the me from home. Raymond in school and Keith out of school. Never mix it up. That was one of the psychic payments, the split-name thing. Anyway, my program soon got me out of 1-4 and into 1-3. I don't remember having a sense of working my way up from the bottom, but I was placed in 2-1 in September 1959—the only African American in the class. Maybe I was getting the brown-stick-around break. I wasn't in the Black-get-back category. During that time, a classmate's mother told her son that I was handsome "for a Negro." I guess people like that could see me as nonthreatening and maybe smooth me into their narrative of America. That wasn't the story on the other side of Junction Boulevard. If anyone in my neighborhood thought me handsome, the judgment came without qualification.

I couldn't worry about all that for-a-Negro business or straighten out anybody's pathology. My main concern was to be on an equal footing with the White kids in class. If they were hiding something, I needed to find it. I was positioned to conform and follow my mother's plan. Not that I wasn't a little rebellious. With a few other classmates, I clowned around. But we didn't become clowns. We had answers in class. We were killing exams. We knew second-grade boundaries.

Reciting the Pledge of Allegiance was mandatory. I found out later that although the school treated the Pledge as an old, sacred tradition, recitation had only been required for a few years. In fact, I was older than the most recent version of the Pledge, the version that includes "under God." America was making things up as it went along, continually modifying the mythology. Line up the Pledge with the story of Myles Standish, the Pilgrim military commander who was deemed heroic and correct for leading a massacre against Native Americans and beheading Wituwamat. Praise valiant George Washington and honest Abraham Lincoln back when students still knew those presidents' actual birthdays. And we saw no reason not to respect President Dwight D. Eisenhower. I also learned important selections from the civic soundtrack—"America the Beautiful" and "My Country, 'Tis of Thee"—even though in assembly I was always and forever off key. Same thing at home when I was trying to be Lloyd Price singing "Personality" or Jackie Wilson doing "Lonely Teardrops."

Baby boomers were the first generation to grow up with nuclear age anxiety. *an unreliable sky holds crackerjack surprises.* The Iron Curtain had been erected, and we were supposedly on the correct side of it. Russians were the enemies. Our side wanted citizen freedom and individual prosperity. Their side opposed freedom and individual prosperity and wanted to fashion the whole world along those lines, by force if necessary. Did they possess the superior weapons if the Cold War turned hot?

It appeared that could be the case, given that the month after I started kindergarten the Russians launched *Sputnik I*, the first artificial satellite. The event sent America into panic because folks figured that the Russians could also be more advanced militarily, possessing better missiles, better bombs. Consequently, America decided to put more pressure on its schools to produce superior math and science students, since theoretically that would address part of the problem: the country's students had fallen behind. We were going to get way more homework than any generation before us, while in school we did civil defense drills. The threat was in the sky, and the sky attracted my attention. I was always interested in and nervous about the space race, in the question, in my mind, of who could get the edge out among the planets and stars.

The first international incident I remember is the Russians shooting down Francis Gary Powers, who was flying a U-2 spy plane for the CIA in the spring of 1960. Powers managed to eject and land with a parachute but fell, along with the spy camera and photographic film, into the hands of the KGB and was eventually sentenced to prison. So that's partly how the second grade ended: Powers shot down by an S-75 surface-to-air missile, seemingly better than anything the United States had. I was on my way to Class 3-1, although my teacher noted in my permanent record, which I was unaware of at the time, that I didn't get along well with other children. That would have been news to me and to Harlem. In any event, I obviously had more to worry about than getting along with the White people around me.

One day I was walking down the block and ran into Lonnie Blair. I'd seen him in school, but we hadn't connected on a deep level. He said he was tougher than I was and asked me how I had gotten my scar. It signaled serious life experience to him. I told him that I got it in a gang fight in Harlem and that he was too young and too little to know about such matters—even though we were the same size and the same age, born within two weeks of each other, as we found out. Lonnie became my main guy at 149 and around the block. He was my primary bridge to the other young brothers I came to know, or maybe I should say earned the right to know. You had to scuffle. Nothing all that vicious at age eight, but you had to put some flesh on the line to get a decent spot in the hierarchy. My style of engagement was a basic bull rush—just launch at the adversary. My father shaped that approach because he was a big

20

wrestling fan and used to experiment with me. He would be down on all fours, and I would charge, trying to attack the best way I knew how. Of course, I always lost. When he grew tired of playing around, he'd simply pin me. He liked watching the staged shows on television and took me to one at Sunnyside Garden Arena. I don't remember the entire card, just the great Wahoo McDaniel in Indian headdress.

The trip to Sunnyside was one of what I call the walking-fast moments because if you hung out with my father, you had to move swiftly. I remember some days in Central Park, where he went to help coach the church softball team. Some moments were at Coney Island. Some down Northern Boulevard to the barbershop. Some to Yankee Stadium. Some later to Shea Stadium. One time we had climbed to the platform of the Junction Boulevard station to catch the Number 7 train. My father gave me the only piece of his advice that I recall from the early years. As we looked down at the track, he warned me never to pee on the third rail because I would be electrocuted.

Lonnie and I met up at Junction Park a lot. That's where he explained to me that we should become blood brothers and how to do it. We each pricked a finger with a pin and then rubbed them together, mingling our blood. That made our friendship more solid than any other, and we had to have each other's back forever. I'm not sure if this was before my baptism or after. I just know the commitments were adding up. I told Lonnie that he should try to get into Class 3-1. I figured he was smart enough. But he wasn't interested at all, even if the maneuver were possible. He said that could only be a problem.

My biggest one in 3-1 was playing myself into some silly White boy–White girl feud. Guys were working out some identity issues and hopped up on the diplomacy talk in the news. They worked up some treaty they wanted the girls to sign. I can't even recall what there was to sign a treaty about. Anyway, the girls thought the whole thing simple-minded, which prompted the boys to ask me to get one of the girls they designated a leader, Susan, to sign it. Accordingly, feeling important, I blocked her path after school as she headed home, further into Jackson Heights, and offered her the document. She walked right around me. It was a blur from there. I punched her in the eye; she staggered one way; I ran the other way toward Corona; she called me a bastard. I had made my greatest public mistake, one that was going to cost me big. I thought of home first. There was leeway about behavior in that space, with the understanding that you never embarrass my mother outside the home. You certainly didn't want her to be forced to take a morning off from work to come address some foolishness at school.

I was fidgety all the next day until Mr. Price finally summoned me to his office to receive what I thought might be the decision to expel me. Susan was with him, looking even more stern than he was. The principal asked me if this was what I learned at home. I knew what he meant: did the moral law laid down at home justify my action? I was correct to reply no on that count. Susan said the boys made me do it. Then Mr. Price went on about discipline and cooperation and learning how to be a gentleman. And he lectured about the need for an apology, which I readily offered. The proceedings concluded once I vowed never to behave in such a manner again. Maybe this was another brown-stick-around break. I couldn't keep counting on those. Susan and I were in the same class for three more years, sometimes working together on school projects and meeting at her home. She became a friend, and I never got caught up in such nonsense again in school or out. I certainly never had reason for another visit to Mr. Price.

One morning on the way to school, I was walking on some cobblestones that ran along the outer boundary of the schoolyard fence. I avoided the sidewalk as I gingerly picked my way along. Unbeknownst to me, Mr. Price was approaching from behind on the sidewalk. He bellowed, "A rugged individualist. I like that." I didn't know fully what he meant, how he was defining me. However, it sounded like something difficult to be, more difficult than picking my way along cobblestones.

I would not have traded my good fortune for a New York Yankees victory over the Pirates in the World Series, although I probably would have considered the proposition if given the chance. That's how serious the sport was. I loved baseball by then, slept with a ball and glove and transistor radio in my bed most nights during the season. Played hardball or softball every chance I got. Collected cards. Watched what games I could on television. Pushed to go to the stadium, something my mother never delivered on back then, although she shared my love of the game. Perhaps I got my passion from her. But she absolutely hated the Yankees. She bled Brooklyn Dodgers blue until they scurried to the West Coast. With the Giants, my father's team, also gone, I simply rooted for the home team, the only team left in town. I *needed* that win but couldn't obtain it if my mother had any power over the situation, which I believe she did. I think she hexed the Yankees because she talked so badly about them. Her negative commentary and the Pirates' win literally drove me to tears.

My mother didn't explain that she was a National League fan because she saw it, as did many, as the civil rights league. On the other hand, the Yankees, along with the Red Sox, were as racist as baseball got. I didn't know that the same year I was born Jackie Robinson, still an active player, called the Yankees racist for still having an all-White roster. They declined to sign Willie Mays. That you don't do. Even Mickey Mantle, New York's pride and joy, was no Willie Mays. Team executives reportedly said they didn't want high-end ticket holders from Westchester County to be forced to sit in a crowd with niggers. I didn't have all that information when I was eight. In 1960 the Yankees had Elston Howard and Hector Lopez. I could find no fault with those choices.

When my mother was eighty-nine years old, I took her to a Mets-Yankees game at Citi Field. By then she had long saved my baseball soul for the Metropolitans. Dressed in her Mets jersey and cap, she turned around and started razzing some Yankees fans seated in the row behind us, clad in their team's merchandise. Somewhat amused, they looked at sixty-four-year-old me and asked if I felt as anti-Yankees as my mother did. She answered for me, confiding that I had been a wayward child but learned.

That and much more. Later in the school term my mother went to a parent-teacher conference one evening, which was nothing for me to worry about because I had school on lock. My language arts were tight. Some of my little essays, some solar system stuff, were displayed on the bulletin board outside the classroom. They were the first writings of mine that I recall being made public. If the parent-teacher conference were about showing off, I was covered. The school had a remedial reading room on the third floor that I was in no danger of having to visit. My math was generally excellent. I'm home listening to something like Chubby Checker and doing the twist. I'm good.

My mother startled me when she returned from the school, grabbed the iron from the kitchen, and started lashing at me with the cord. When I think of all the people I know who were punished with that type of cord, I don't know why companies just didn't just sell them as a separate item. That's how popular they were. However, you don't think about marketing when you are getting flamed by an ironing cord across your back, legs, arms, buttocks. You don't even think about nuclear stuff. "So you fighting girls in school?" I denied it until she reminded me about Susan. That was like Juneteenth in reverse. The official news arrives late, and you get your ass beat. Even though I had a deal with the principal, I think my teacher dimed me out. I think I was supposed to be a Pygmalion in that class and that my teacher possessed some distrust that it could really happen or should even be the goal. I was in good academic shape, more than satisfactory all around, but she noted on my permanent record card that I needed improvement in social living because I occasionally resented control (a constant for me throughout elementary school) and occasionally evaded responsibility (usually meaning not doing homework that I already knew the answer to). "The parent-child relationship seems disturbed," according to one entry. In June 1961, the negative narrative reached its apex. Two simple sentences under the heading Outstanding Disabilities: "Father not living with family. Raymond needs supervision."

4

Newspapers indicated that the whole world needed supervision. Nikita Khrushchev, no elementary school kid but first secretary of the Central Committee of the Communist Party of the Soviet Union, banged his shoe on his desk in the General Assembly at the United Nations (supervision). His ace cosmonaut Yuri Gagarin became the first human in outer space, orbiting the earth in only eighty-nine minutes. The Russians were miles ahead in space technology, and their weapons technology couldn't be lagging much behind. The Alan B. Shepard flight, a suborbital move that lasted only fifteen minutes, comprised a weak response, especially since it occurred a year later than originally scheduled because of technical difficulties. Nor was Gus Grissom as impressive as Gagarin. His flight was also suborbital, and the spacecraft sank when the hatch door blew off. A crew rescued Grissom, and I dutifully applauded the overall effort, but NASA really needed to get its act together (supervision). France making noise testing atomic bombs. I didn't know French politics, but the experiments seemed scary and needed to be kept in check (supervision). America sending troops to Vietnam while my Uncle Harold, the youngest of my mother's three brothers, enlisted in the Marines. Harold used to be at our house with his chest expander and other exercise equipment. He also practiced a false baritone that he thought he might use when he worked in radio one day. One of my heroes. Better look out for him (supervision). John F. Kennedy was in office, as my mother and most of my classmates had wished, but that didn't stop the CIA from orchestrating the execution of Patrice Lumumba in the Congo. The CIA, screwing up in Cuba as well and having 80 percent of the invasion force captured in the fiasco at the Bay of Pigs. The agency was out of control (supervision). And building an eighty-seven-mile wall to divide Germany into East and West couldn't make the most sense (supervision).

The Freedom Riders fanned out across the South on buses in attempts to defeat Jim Crow. I had some concept of their endeavors from the papers and the racial banter in Harlem and Corona barbershops. The first politician I remember being aware of was arch-segregationist Strom Thurmond. Since my Harlem days, his name had come up frequently for pulling one racist maneuver or another, and he became my immediate reference for all that was wrong in the South. I eagerly followed the morality play: *The Good Guys against the Forces of Strom Thurmond*. I had an incipient sense of northern segregation. Black zones and White zones were familiar distinctions to me by then. I experienced them. On the other hand, the southern situation remained largely cerebral to me. I did have family connections—Grandma (maternal), Grandma Rosie (paternal), Aunt Vandella (youngest of the three sisters), Uncle Aaron (Grandma's second husband and Vandella's father), and several cousins. I had only been to the South once that I recall, an eighteen-hour journey on the train to Waycross, Georgia, where Uncle Aaron picked us up for the seventy-mile ride to Ocilla. I don't remember much about the train or trains. Pat remembers one was the *West Coast Champion*. Because we traveled along the eastern coast, her recollection seemed strange to me until I learned that the name referred to the route taken once the train made it past Georgia to Florida. The *West Coast Champion* proceeded down the west coast of Florida while the *East Coast Champion* went the other way. In any case, I don't recall where we sat or what kind of people were around us. I probably slept most of the way. I know we had our good, trusty, traveling chicken to eat, but other than that I don't remember anything about dining arrangements or restroom customs on board or in depots. In Ocilla, the houses were on stilts with black wash pots in front. I took castor oil administered by Grandma and went up the road to play with my cousin Alfred, who brought all his clothes out onto the front porch in the morning to get dressed. I don't recall any peculiar race dynamics, though my great-grandmother, Georgia Jackson, looked White.

The Freedom Riders revealed to me the social landscape and the idea of a civil rights movement associated with CORE, SNCC, and the SCLC. I was introduced to James Farmer, John Lewis, Diane Nash, and Martin Luther King Jr. The crackers, as said in the barbershop, the Strom Thurmond–like crackers, disregarded federal law and formed attack mobs populated largely with local police and the Ku Klux Klan. They firebombed buses and beat Freedom Riders unconscious with iron pipes. Birmingham's police commissioner, Bull Connor, was a key villain.

26

I heard mixed reviews of the Kennedy administration, which tried to be half pregnant in its response. Reluctantly, partly due to international criticism, including from the Russians, the Kennedys cut deals whereby state police and National Guard units would protect protesters during rides. On the flip side, they would not intervene when protesters were arrested for violating local segregation laws regarding water fountains, bathrooms, and lunch counters. The Kennedys still garnered decent support in the barbershop. However, it was nothing to take for granted. They needed to work harder (supervision).

I guess the main thing for me was that I had cleared the hump, that is, made it past the third grade and gathered momentum. I often visited the branch of the Queens Public Library on 81st Street. That was about a mile into Jackson Heights, on the next block from the Jewish Center, about as far as I wandered into that neighborhood during those days. Not that I felt it was dangerous. Just not much interesting to see, with block after block of apartment buildings. 82nd Street, a stop on the Number 7 train, was busy with commerce. But there was nothing down that way for me except the library. I would sample the popular juvenile books: *Black Beauty*, Nancy Drew and Hardy Boys tales, Clair Bee's Chip Hilton sports series. Although all in on Chip, I wasn't sure about Bee. You didn't expect to find Black heroes at the library, so I was all right with White boy Chip, who seemed a combination of Jerry West, Johnny Unitas, and Babe Ruth. He could drop forty points on the hardwood and captain a football team to the state championship. He could go to a college baseball tournament, get off the plane, and throw a no-hitter—and be generous enough to teach a Japanese kid how to throw one also and beat the U.S. squad. Chip was even nice with his hands, possessed courage, and treated everybody, including Black people, with respect. Notwithstanding, author Bee didn't really know what to do with Black characters. A "big Negro kid" could play basketball or football well but couldn't talk much, if at all, or even have a name in a Claire Bee book. No, Chip Hilton was a dose of White heroism, which was all you realistically could expect. You accepted him the same way you accepted Superman, who was a guy from another galaxy but hardly looked like it. He looked more like midwesterner Dick Tracy, who held down the front cover of the *Daily News* Sunday comics section.

Concerning comics, I was mostly a DC guy. Marvel played big with students in my junior high school, but by then I wasn't reading comic books. In elementary school I focused on the Krypton folks as well as Flash, J'onn J'onnz, and Green Lantern. I found out later that Amiri Baraka was also a fan of Green Lantern. My sisters read comic books also—Little Dot, Little Lotta, Archie, and Richie Rich. More unreality. I checked in on those characters because they were in the house.

My favorite action, though, took place on PS 149's playground. Why let Chip Hilton top me? Any sport would do—basketball, handball, stickball, punch ball, softball, running races, touch football. I loved them all. Maybe I had the most potential in football, the game that, in December of my fourth-grade term, brought me my first major injury.

At dismissal time one day I was so eager to get out of the classroom that I bolted from my seat and banged my knee into the side of the desk. The joint swelled a bit, but that didn't keep me from a football game on the playground. After my knee grew worse during the game, my solution was to go home and rub alcohol on it. The next day the knee swelled more, and I limped through the school day. By night I could barely walk. I struggled up the stairs to the second floor, where my father stayed in a room separate from the main apartment. He needed only a quick glance before deciding to grab a cab to Physicians Hospital, a little more than two miles straight down 34th Avenue, where Intermediate School 230 now stands. Turns out that I had a fracture in my kneecap, which kept me in traction for most of the month. I'm not even sure I had known the word *fracture*, but it was my circumstance. I also went in with a fever of 106 degrees. My father asked nervously how high fevers can go. The doctor replied matter-of-factly, "This is about it."

My mother came to visit every day after work. She usually brought fruit and a newspaper. Sometimes she brought a sports magazine. I read about Floyd Patterson defeating Tom McNeeley, though everybody knew that Patterson couldn't protect the heavyweight title against Sonny Liston. Liston was my number one sports idol, the terror with the fourteen-inch fists. You had to respect that power and huge reputation. Mantle was high up on the list, of course. Also Wilt Chamberlain, who had just squared off against Elgin Baylor and the Los Angeles Lakers and scored a record seventy-eight points in one game. Baylor, a fellow idol, scored sixty-three. Style wise, I tried to imitate Oscar Robertson's shot. Robertson sort of cocked it back to shoot, a slingshot type of motion. This worked better for me because, at the age of nine, I lacked the strength to shoot it straight on as I later did. I moved my release to the side, behind my ear, sort of how Jamaal Wilkes would shoot it. Rounding out my first-team lineup of sports heroes was Wilma Rudolph, the darling, at least for me, of the 1960 Olympics, and the New York Giants overall, although they were no threat to vanquish the Green Bay Packers. They needed somebody like the incomparable Jim Brown or Heisman Trophy winner Ernie Davis, and even that might not have been enough.

I read about Adolf Eichmann being sentenced to death for war crimes. This case greatly interested my classmates. In their structures of feeling, Eichmann represented a nightmare, a symbol of a still possible threat, one greater, they tried to convince me, than anti-Black racism. They argued to me that if Germany had won the war, they would be in concentration camps, and I would be lucky to be a Negro. Obviously, the logic was twisted. The Negro had never been lucky in America no matter who won wars. But in those days I had plenty of time and patience to ponder the question.

And my mother wasn't pushing me down. That's a memory from a few years before when I had my tonsils removed. While the anesthesia was wearing off, I was penned in a hospital bed behind bars and struggling to get out. My mother kept pushing me down onto the mattress until I gave up. No bars this time. No struggle. No restraint. She fingered my knee carefully, and we talked about micro-local news. How the hospital was. What my sisters were doing as well as Aunt Vandella and my little cousin Carolyn, who had come up from Georgia to stay with us. I was curious about the block in general, whether there were any more fights between our neighbor and his three sons. He would drink and start beating his wife over some alleged infraction. I imagine this had transpired for years. But his sons were pretty much grown by then and would triple-team him, which they needed to do because he was a big strong man. The brawls would spill out onto the sidewalk; the sons were like lions trying to take down a grown wildebeest, circling, avoiding danger, and looking for the best chance for one of them to leap in from behind for a takedown. It was doable but not easy.

I wondered about some of my routines. Barbara and I used to go to this woman's house a couple of blocks down the avenue to write letters that she would dictate to us. My mother, offering us as literate and capable, arranged this. Barbara went first and came home with a dollar or two; then I got in on it. Sometimes I went by myself. I remember the house being neat but kind of dark with a lot of old-style furniture. On some visits the woman would have us work on a word puzzle that appeared in the *Long Island Press*. You were given word pairs and had to choose the word that best fit the sentences. You mailed in your entry, and if you got them all correct you could win money. I don't recall her ever winning, but we were paid either way.

At home, Barbara and I, and later Pat, would work on our knowledge. We had the *World Book Encyclopedia*. My mother was a salesperson's dream when it came to stuff like that. She didn't mind plunging into debt if she thought it helped us in school. We would choose different volumes and take turns reading entries, leaving out the title, until another one of us guessed the entry. For example, if you were holding the Q volume and read "is a borough in New York City," that would be one of the simple ones.

As part of a school program, my mother sent Barbara and me to the Boulevard Theatre down in Jackson Heights to see plays on Saturday mornings. Movies were the main fare at the Boulevard by the 1960s. But unlike most movie houses, it had been designed to be primarily a venue for plays and musicals. We saw several, including the most memorable, *Snow White and the Seven Dwarfs*. I have always had room for fairy tales.

My father came by the hospital a few times with more fruit and more magazines. His visits were briefer. Quick male stuff: How you feeling? Treating you all right? Nothing heavy, maybe a sports tidbit. But I still admired him. I remembered his sitting in a chair at home while I was on the floor beside him working on a math problem that he had given me. He made it to a parents' observation day, the only Black person among the parents who stood in the back of the classroom to watch us. He backed me when I went to retrieve my baseball glove from a boy (later a good friend) who had stolen it because I hadn't kept close enough watch on it in the schoolyard. He'd swim way out at Coney Island, so far that we could barely see him. Once he came into the schoolyard wearing white painter's bib overalls smeared with paint. He had been working on a house with a friend and, riding around with him, had spotted me shooting baskets with schoolmates. He asked for the ball and shot a couple of old-fashioned hook shots. He said that was the way to do it. I told him that people didn't play that style of basketball anymore because it was corny. He watched me hit and miss some shots; then he hit a few more hooks, each from a little farther out. I didn't even know he could shoot.

I worried a great deal about my mother. I knew she was no super-woman even if she had super moments. Unsure about what I could do, if anything, to help the situation, I merely brooded. I had no answer for the Shirelles. After all, who knows who will still love whom tomorrow? In any event, on December 23, as my fears about being hospitalized on Christmas mounted, I was discharged to my father. My equilibrium was off. After getting dressed, I impatiently hopped off the bed and imme-diately collapsed to the floor. I had to be taken down in a wheelchair. However, I quickly recovered.

5

Two months later, I barely made it past my front door before I was attacked. Lonnie showed up with about six or seven young brothers from the neighborhood to beat me down. They punched me in my chest, arms, and legs. When I defensively dropped to the cold pavement, they pounded my back. I loved it. The licks were one of our rituals. *We don't care what you do in that classroom with them White kids. You do enough— scraps, foot races, signifyin, lyin, soundin, joanin—on this side of Junction Boulevard to be one of us. Happy birthday.* I made it to my feet, ten years old, exaggerating the pain I was in. Then we melted into the Saturday afternoon on our side of the line.

On the other side, I stayed pretty much in step, clapping with my classmates in the school auditorium when John Glenn circled the globe at seventeen thousand miles per hour. Mr. Price said it took him longer to get to work than the ninety minutes it took Glenn to make one orbit. That didn't seem quite right to me, but I accepted the story. President Kennedy declared that Glenn and the other astronauts were Americans of whom we should be proud. He didn't say anything about those "hidden figures" who were not publicized until decades later in Margot Lee Shetterly's book and the subsequent movie. Glenn wouldn't fly without checking the trajectory calculations with African American mathematician Katherine Johnson. In school, we had no idea. Kennedy said space was the new ocean that we had to sail. Americans could not sail it first, he acknowledged, while also stating that Americans could sail it best. He aimed to land a man on the moon before Russia could achieve the feat.

Our teacher, Mrs. Kaufmann, pushed us to explore on the page our responses to the space race. We had another chance to make the bulletin board. I chose to write a poem, producing some stanzas about my imagined travels to the moon, Mars, and so on. I concluded, *But no matter how far I roam / I'll always want to come back home / Where the atmosphere is always glad / With my three sisters and Mom and Dad.* That was weird. I didn't even use words like "Mom" and "Dad." Well, maybe I did on that side of the line. As the scholar R. A. Hudson asserts, every speech utterance can be viewed as an "act of identity in multi-dimensional space." So "Mom" and "Dad" it had to be, even though I was a "Ma" or "Moms" type and don't recall ever addressing my father during that time by any name. Later it was "Pops," not "Dad."

I made the bulletin board again. Mrs. Kaufmann called me up to her desk and told me I had a good rhythmic sense. I suppose Dr. Seuss had something to do with that. I had absorbed his work and added it to my verbal storehouse. Overall, I just followed my ear. That term, she recommended Ogden Nash and Langston Hughes, and I was all for their humor. Nash was all about rhyme, which I figured was an essential element of poetry. His humor and innovation were readily apparent, but he relied on old-fashioned content with that baseball poem "Line-up for Yesterday." I knew "yesterday" was his point, but that meant no Jackie Robinson, Don Newcombe (a particular favorite of my mother), Roy Campanella, Willie Mays, Ernie Banks, Frank Robinson, or Roberto Clemente. Not even Ted Williams or Stan Musial or Mickey Mantle. I didn't mind commentary about the likes of Babe Ruth, Lou Gehrig, Ty Cobb, Rogers Hornsby, Walter Johnson, and Cy Young. I knew of them all. However, I had more interest in contemporary lineups and experimented with a few Mays-Banks-Robinson-Clemente pieces.

I found Hughes to be funny also, but he slipped in a lot of serious moments. I read "The Ballad of the Landlord" a couple of years before Jonathan Kozol exposed his African American fourth graders in Boston to the poem and was fired for doing so. School officials explained that they could not endorse literature written in bad grammar or native dialects because their mission involved trying to disrupt the speech patterns of the students and get them to speak properly. Reading "The Ballad of the Landlord," the argument went, would entrench speech patterns the school wanted to break. Of course, poems in Standardized English ain't breaking nobody's native speech pattern, and nobody's native speech pattern need be broken by no school system no way. All that psychological and social warfare aimed at those kids made no sense, educationally or otherwise. As sociolinguist Peter Trudgill explains, language eradication is wrong because it conveys messages of inferiority, which can cause alienation from school or rejection of the home group.

I read the poem in the library, not in class. My teacher faced no jeopardy. Neither did I if the issue was just about language. My parents were pushing, Jewish kids were pulling, and I would be all right in the sorting game. But it *was* a sorting game and not set up for everyone to become upwardly mobile. Teachers could have good intentions and can help some, but institutions are more powerful and can disable many. I was moving from top class to top class. However, Lonnie and the crew weren't, and nobody ever asks about them.

Strangely—at least everyone tells me it's strange—I was fascinated most by Hughes's "Suicide's Note": "The calm / Cool face of the river / Asked me for a kiss." I was enchanted, not by the idea of suicide but by what poetry could be. It didn't have to rhyme, although I still liked rhyme. And rivers could ask for kisses. Metaphor was the thing, kind of like in the street. You let meanings collide. In fact, there were collisions everywhere.

During this time weeks could pass without us seeing our father. We could catch him upstairs sporadically. Much later, he told me that his gambling had grown worse, absolutely no cooperation from the horses. Despite seeing what it was costing him, he couldn't stop. At least that was the narrative he shared. My mother wasn't saying much that I remember. Over the years she never spoke too harshly about him. She calmly called him selfish or stupid. That's about it. Once, during a court proceeding related to their legal separation, a proceeding during which he didn't acknowledge us, she told him, "You're going to need these kids one day." But she never tried to turn us against him, never tried to block us from seeing him—if we could. She needed no "anti" campaign. She sincerely hoped that, even though not with her, he would step up his parenting because that could only be good for us.

My aunt went back to Georgia, and I stopped going to church. For a long time I didn't think the events were related, but now I see them as links in a chain of stress for my mother during the spring and summer of 1962. My aunt would be fine, but my mother, sort of a parent to her, given the fifteen-year age difference, had a vision for her in New York that would remain unfulfilled. My mother's resistance was down when I began nagging her about why we continued to worship in Harlem. This meant at least an hour on the subway to get there, Sunday school, main service, waiting on my mother to finish with day care, sometimes

Baptist Training Union in the evening, on occasion visiting friends farther up the hill on Amsterdam Avenue. Seemed like too much to me. I remained on board with the sentiment of John 3:16, the first verse I ever memorized, but how was the everyday stuff going to be straightened out? Not, I surmised, by being up in Harlem all day every Sunday and missing game after game—whether televised or ones I wanted to play in. I badgered my mother so much that she finally asked me one day if I knew how to get home. This was simple. I had paid attention to all the stops and to where we changed trains. When I detailed the route, she gave me a token, some change, and the key to the house. Today the child welfare people might get on the case of someone who sent a ten-year-old from borough to borough on the subway. Anyway, that was my departure from Convent Avenue Baptist. It wasn't long before no one in my family attended church with any regularity.

In September James Meredith, a U.S. Air Force veteran, attempted to desegregate the University of Mississippi. That was his right, and the courts backed him as he tried to exercise it against the wishes of university officials and Governor Ross Barnett. I began to link Barnett with Strom Thurmond. It took the federal government, mainly meaning President Kennedy and Attorney General Robert Kennedy, to get Meredith in school, and to do that they had to bring in the National Guard to quell a riot by Whites, who destroyed property and attacked police. I didn't understand why Meredith bothered. I knew about racial prejudice and about his constitutional rights. I agreed with Meredith's moves. My reservation had to do with whether the outcome justified the effort.

The men in the barbershop on Northern Boulevard, up around 100th Street, which was about as far eastward on the Boulevard as I ventured during those days, expressed decidedly more militance. They never tired of expounding on the evildoing of crackers, people who never meant Black folks any good. The men compellingly spoke on a series of racist incidents and policies, and on ineffectual legislation all over the country. They provided more context and exhibited more emotion than was evident in discussions at school. Their implied motto: To dismantle White supremacy, no crackers get no breaks no time. Moreover, they made sure I knew that crackers weren't confined to the South; they were all over the North, including in Jackson Heights, right across Junction Boulevard.

My mother would not have disputed the claims of the men in the barbershop. However, she would not have fixated on them. We never heard anti-White declarations in our home. Her view was that every group contained good and bad. She thought that if we were exposed to a healthy range of experiences and perspectives, we would figure things out. Especially concerning me, it seemed her unstated directive was always to *handle it*. Display more self-control in school—*had better do that*—and *handle it*.

She had a copy of *Black Like Me* on her nightstand. The title caught me because of Langston Hughes's "Dream Variations." Langston's simile: "Night coming tenderly / Black like me." The author of the book, John Howard Griffin, was a White man—a Texas cracker, according to the men in the barbershop—who, with the help of a dermatologist and a tanning lamp, darkened his skin and traveled through the South for weeks pretending to be a Negro so he could see what it was like for Negroes down there. I couldn't suspend disbelief because I couldn't imagine Griffin fooling many people. It seemed almost comical, like people not being able to see that Clark Kent is Superman. Besides, we had better texts— Richard Wright's *Black Boy* for one, more Langston Hughes poems for others—that portrayed southern race relations. The read was interesting, though, better than the movie. When my mother took us to see it, I could only laugh at the idea that James Whitmore was supposed to be Black. He didn't look the part, act the part, or sound the part. The native of White Plains, New York—and Yale graduate—didn't even sound like a White man from Texas, which was the role. I don't recall discussing either the book or the film at any length with my mother. I suppose exposure was enough for her. She also took us to see the film versions of *A Raisin in the Sun* and *To Kill a Mockingbird*. She always did like Sidney Poitier and Gregory Peck (and James Arness of *Gunsmoke* and Vince Edwards of *Ben Casey*, by the way). Those trips were less about sociology and politics, and more about just being a kid. I identified with my age peer Scout.

I studied my classmates more intently, trying to detect signs of cracker qualities. I pondered their responses to me in class. Those seemed to be in order, given that I received invitations to parties and a get-well card while in the hospital. I visited some of their homes to wait on them to change clothes to go to the park or hang out by their buildings or play board games such as Monopoly and Stratego. I didn't have to go home immediately after school. I met their siblings and their parents, all of whom were welcoming. Not many other Black kids were walking around the Southridge Co-ops. I think Johnny Terrell lived there. The world would know him as the actor John Canada Terrell from movies such as *She's Gotta Have It*, *Boomerang*, and *The Five Heartbeats*. Or that classic *Hey Love* television commercial. "No, my brother. You've got to buy your own." I never knew him that well, although I think he was in Barbara's class. I mostly saw him on the playground during lunch recess or while he was playing for a local softball team. I joined with some of my classmates to form our own squad, the Monarchs—ironic because I didn't yet know about the Kansas City Monarchs and Cool Papa Bell, Satchel Paige, or Buck O'Neil. What I buried until a classmate reminded me years later is that the team used our basement as a clubhouse. At first I doubted his recollection. I couldn't fathom that these White boys had come across the dividing line to my house. Not to mention that our basement was not finished. But he provided details, such as our trip together down Junction Boulevard to get decals—the letter M—to iron onto our caps. That jogged my memory. We had no jerseys because we weren't in a league. We hustled up games, sort of barnstorming in Jackson Heights and Elmhurst.

Marty Rosenberger was my best friend among the Jews. A kind of a clumsy guy with thick glasses but plenty of spirit and hustle, he was always ready for softball or touch football. His home was my most frequent destination in Jackson Heights. I would even visit him on weekends to watch games on television. Marty helped me find a cracker. On the playground during a game of touch, a classmate claimed I hadn't tagged him when I knew I had. I guess he wanted badly to prevail and was frustrated that he hardly ever did over me. We went back and forth on the call, normal schoolyard stuff. He wanted to choose me for it, a common resolution. I declined, certain that I had tagged him. Then he casually called me a nigger, a filthy cheating nigger. Wow. Never completely discount the men in the barbershop. Here was a Jew with cracker in him up in the North. I hit him with a quick two piece and more. As he was retreating, running from the park, Marty clipped him on the side of his head. I wasn't worried about this making it to Mr. Price.

The apology came to me this time. Lonnie thought the ending was perfect. His blood brother continued to prove righteous even if he entertained those White boys a bit too much. Lonnie went on a rant about Jews. I left out the part about Rosenberger.

6

The men in the barbershop discussed the Birmingham campaign, pointing out that many of the children who skipped school to march were my age. I never missed school unless sick. George Wallace, governor of Alabama, had already made the team with his declaration of "segregation now, segregation tomorrow, segregation forever." Now Bull Connor, head of the police in Birmingham, the infamous "Bombingham," became a segregation all-star with his show of force—billy clubs, German shepherds, and high-pressure hoses—to shut down demonstrations. Police went so far as to jail Martin Luther King Jr. All this proved to most men in the barbershop the wrongheadedness of nonviolent protest and of integration. The conversation ran in favor of the pronouncements of Malcolm X, who lived in our neighborhood, the East Elmhurst side, and criticized the quest for integration and tactics such as marching to ask for rights and pushing children out front to be brutalized and arrested. This discourse put me in a trick bag because "integration" had a positive ring for me. It was a synonym for equal rights. The men in the barbershop warned me to keep the focus on rights, not integration. You didn't need integration to have rights. You didn't need to be accepted by anybody because they weren't better than you in the first place. What you wanted was justice and that equal money. While they respected Reverend Shuttlesworth and had no problem with his agitating for employment opportunities for Blacks, and didn't disagree with desegregation efforts, they had little or no faith in marches to effect fundamental change.

I never believed my classmates were better than me. My mother made it impossible for me to believe that. They were coming to a clubhouse in *our* basement. What I wanted was to be in the mix if big opportunities were down the line. Whatever the gold turned out to be, I wanted to be qualified and eligible to get it. I didn't have to call that mission integration.

38

It wasn't going to work anyway. Around that time, 130 students were transferred from Junior High School 127 in East Elmhurst to Junior High School 141 in Astoria, a mostly White enclave several miles away. Black students, if caught in small groups, were often chased from the school area by gangs. On one occasion, three White teenagers subdued a twelve-year-old Black boy and painted his face white. That was integration. A teacher named Helen Marshall, who lived in East Elmhurst, headed a committee that reported these incidents to Superintendent Calvin Gross and Mayor Robert Wagner. The men in the barbershop were not impressed. They were more intrigued with the case of William Moore, who was better than John Howard Griffin. This was a White man, a former Marine with a good post office job, being openly against Jim Crow in Jim Crow territory. A member of the Baltimore chapter of CORE, he planned a four-hundred-mile solo protest walk along Highway 11 from Chattanooga, Tennessee, across Alabama, on to Jackson, Mississippi, wearing signs like "End Segregation in America." It was a noble but crazy stunt. He came nowhere close and, barely into Alabama, was found on the side of the road with two bullets in his head.

The men in the barbershop hadn't been as interested in the Cuban Missile Crisis, deciding all along that someone would back down. The more likely threat was unfolding in Queens as the Con Edison power company tried to place a nuclear plant, which would have been the world's largest, on the Queens side of the East River, near the geographical center of New York City and only four miles from my home. The utility company dismissed objections, but locals felt the threat of radiation to be very real and, despite moments of high anxiety, the activists eventually prevailed.

Poems began to flow more, including an adventure piece about Clupzitzobop, which sounds like a Thelonious Monk or Dizzy Gillespie or Charlie Parker title. The poems are lost, unfortunately, but I produced enough to be associated with that activity. My fifth-grade teacher, besides bestowing upon me a general rating of "Excellent," made a simple entry on my school record under Guidance Data and the category Outstanding Interests: "Poetry—Creative writing."

I wrote a poem after my last trip to Coney Island with my mother and sisters. It began, "On Stillwell Avenue in Brooklyn Town" and went on to describe in rhyme everything we did that day along with social commentary about what could screw up a pleasant day like that. We were with Rita and Mark, a West Indian couple who lived on Eastern Parkway in the Crown Heights section of Brooklyn, between Nostrand and Rogers. Rita worked with my mother in Lower Manhattan. The first time we visited them, Barbara and I walked over to Nostrand and ran into what seemed like a throng of Quakers to us but were Hasidim, which my mother, Rita, and Mark had to explain to us. At any rate, Mark, who had a patient and engaging demeanor, really took an interest in that Coney Island poem. He maintained that I had to keep writing, advice I followed sporadically.

James Joyce wrote, "The supreme question about a work of art is out of how deep a life does it spring." I doubt we should be asking supreme questions about the poetry of eleven-year-olds. On the other hand, it seems my life grew increasingly deep for a kid. For example, why did I have to solve the Huck Finn problem? Our teacher read to us from an unabridged version of Twain's novel and asked me if I opposed her being faithful to the text and saying "nigger." All eyes were on me, the only African American in my class—for the fourth straight year. I imagine that if I hadn't been there, the issue wouldn't have been raised. The teacher and pupils would have just niggered their way on through the text. But it fell to me, someone cut off from home and the barbershop at that precise moment and not fully prepared to analyze the situation, to set the agenda. *And perhaps not spoil the party? What really is the party in my absence?* I said I had no objection and wasn't bothered, though I was troubled by the whole scenario. My mother would just say handle it. Role-play how you need to role-play and handle it. And behave.

Things grew deeper. My mother did not know that my father had not been paying the mortgage. Apparently, the arrangement they had was that he would. She only became aware of his omission when the truck from the oil company arrived to make a delivery. When my mother informed the driver that she had not yet ordered any oil, the man responded that the new owner had placed the order. That's how we found out about our imminent eviction. The ensuing days are fuzzy to me, how we packed and relocated. That's one of two events in my early life that I should remember in more detail, or so it seems to me. As you know, I have vivid memories of many earlier occurrences. But I remain blank about the move, probably the most significant event for my family at that point relative to class or demographic position or dreams. Even Mrs. Handle It had to be devastated. She had played it correctly by the age of thirty-six, secured the home to build equity and avoid a lifetime of paying rent. Now that prospect appeared to be gone.

We ended up about a half mile to the east, farther into the territory on our side of Junction Boulevard. We were on 32nd Avenue, one block north of Northern Boulevard, instead of being, as we had been, one block to the south. Our apartment, with rent higher than the mortgage payments had been, was on the first floor of a two-family residence. I had a walk of fourteen blocks to school instead of two, although that wasn't so bad in the warm weather of May. I no longer had my own room but had to share one with Pat. She remained feisty but could be shut down. All you had to do was wait for *Alfred Hitchcock* to come on. She wasn't bad when she heard the beginning of the opening theme from Charles Gounod's "Funeral March of a Marionette." Pat would jump in bed, tuck her head under the covers, and be fast asleep before the music stopped playing. Nothing else ever scared her like that. Recently, she called and asked me to guess what she had been watching. Not in my universe of guesses would I have picked *Alfred Hitchcock*. I truly couldn't believe it.

My immediate task was to negotiate the unfamiliar streets, especially the ones with which I would most identify, 32nd Avenue, 105th Street, and 104th Street. This is where, after paying the customary pecking-order dues, some of my most enduring friendships, along with an enemyship or two, were formed. In fact, my first day on the block I had a fight that had to be broken up by adults before it got too far. My fellow combatant, predictably, became one of my closest friends.

We still were not in what some would recognize as a physical ghetto. There was "neighborhood deterioration," as one observer commented, due to a weakened tax base and White flight, but there remained a somewhat heterogenous Black character. This wasn't central Harlem, although "Little Harlem" was a reference attached to the area, say, of Northern Boulevard from 112th Street down to Junction. A primary objective for many parents was to keep their kids "off that Boulevard," sometimes simply called "the Bully." Some of us couldn't avoid it because we had to go to school or the store or run errands for our parents or visit friends. As I grew older, I wanted to be on the Boulevard anyway because that's where the action was and that's where you could be certified as being authentically "from Corona." It was as much an attitude as anything else. Several designations, in fact, were and still are in dispute. To be from the other side of Astoria Boulevard, a wide thoroughfare to the north, was to be from East Elmhurst, a more upscale neighborhood that extended northward to LaGuardia Airport. Some, however, consider the area between Northern Boulevard and Astoria Boulevard, which is where I lived, to be part of East Elmhurst and argue vehemently that they are from East Elmhurst, not Corona. As proof they cite the 11369 zip code as opposed to the 11368 zip code. However, that's only post-office logic because East Elmhurst residents campaigned with determination for a new branch and the 69 code. You can find city-planning maps indicating that Astoria Boulevard is the geographical dividing line, which was more socioeconomically accurate. So everybody is right. I wrote my address as an East Elmhurst address and was technically correct to some, but I grew to be "from Corona." In my mind that meant the area from Astoria Boulevard to Roosevelt Avenue to the south and between Junction Boulevard to the east and the Grand Central Parkway to the west. Part of where I landed semantically had to do with street credibility. No matter where you lived, you needed to develop some to be "from Corona."

This meant, in part, figuring out a posture relative to the Enchanters or, more precisely, the Baby Enchanters, because they were in my age range. You could join the gang and perform what that entailed, including adopting a new name. You could largely avoid them, easier to do if you went to PS 149, although you had to cross paths with them in the street sooner or later, possibly on your own block, even if you stayed off the Boulevard. You could mix, if allowed, while remaining a nonmember, which meant you had to stand up for yourself when tested. It was a good idea to be part of a network, not necessarily a gang—the Chaplains were an alternative—in which you were spoken for. You couldn't afford to be, as Baldwin might have articulated it, a stranger in the village.

I managed to stay plain old me while not ducking and hiding but forming enough friendships, some with gang members, not to be a target. However, the key might have been that I was adopted by a few people in older divisions. Beacon, for example, was five years my senior. I was sitting on the stoop while he visited with a girl who lived next door when a guy came pedaling on a bike down the avenue in our direction. Beacon leaped up, ran to the curb, and snapped a car antenna. He took off his jacket and rolled it around his left arm, preparing to defend himself as the newcomer, someone I would come to know well, discarded his bike, popped a blade, and took a few violent swipes. Beacon parried expertly, frustrating the attacker, who hopped back onto his bike and headed back up the avenue while warning, "This ain't over." I hadn't seen that much intensity since I watched our neighbor on 34th Avenue battle his sons. At any rate, Beacon's reputation was solid, I idolized him, and he generally looked out for me. People older than Beacon weren't a problem because I didn't have enough stature to be of value to them. I recall the Chaplains being more numerous but mostly older. The Big Enchanters seemed to be wilder and sometimes had their hands full with country boys, whom we called Bamas, or the Dukes, an Italian gang on the other side of Roosevelt, what we called Corona Heights. In fact, I think the reputation of the Enchanters stemmed from a takeover of sorts at Newtown High School in neighboring Elmhurst in 1961 when they, along with the Chaplains, battled the Dukes. Someone, and it wasn't an Enchanter or Chaplain, got hit in the head with a meat cleaver. As people scattered from the scene, the police scrambled to find suspects. They stopped and boarded buses headed toward Corona, namely, the Q72 on Junction Boulevard. That type of action was altogether too heavy for me. I did enjoy the songs, or toasts, belted out while someone was drumming on a mailbox: *in nineteen hundred and a sixty-one / the young Enchanters had just begun*. The story had twists and turns, such as *look over the mountain and what do I see? / a bad muthafucka name a Stag-o-lee* and *when I grow ol / my balls are col / can't cop me no pussy no mo*.

My father came by a few times until it was determined that I should come to where he lived to pick up child support payments. Of course, this was tricky because I hadn't established many of my contacts yet. My process had to be adequate. When I left him, I would stuff the money into the bottom of one of my socks and tie my shoes or sneakers tight. I kept my pants pockets either empty or with a normal amount of money, which wasn't much. If I got ripped off for a little change, fine. Just never the other.

From what I heard my father raised the question of reconciling. My mother wouldn't even entertain the idea if a house weren't part of the plan. My father reportedly inquired, "That's all it takes? A house? That's nothing." It was not nothing. That house never materialized. My father had enough trouble with child support, missing payments or coming up short on occasion. My sisters and I did appreciate that he gave us allowances a couple of times a month—most months.

I continued to adjust. Talked sports. Celtics won again. Yankees battling the Red Sox, White Sox, and Twins. Cardinals wrestling with the Dodgers and Giants. Cassius Clay talking too much after beating Harlem's Doug Jones, of whom I was a fan—my old home team preferred over the Olympics upstart. Played stickball, ran the foot races, participated in the signifyin. I was a minority on the block in terms of not having a father around, so I took a little grief about that. Nearly all of us had connections to the South and expressed concern about the progress or lack thereof regarding the civil rights movement. We were collectively shading toward militance. What was the March on Washington against the murder of Medgar Evers in his driveway?

7

Denise McNair was my age. The fact served as one of my takeaways from the bombing of the 16th Street Baptist Church in Birmingham, which occurred about a week after we returned to school for the sixth grade. Black girls slaughtered, including an eleven-year-old, and no get-back. Not that I thought revenge the best option in every case. I was always a nervous sort of kid who could imagine the worst outcome of any conflict. Get-back after get-back until everybody had been annihilated. My imagination, conditioned by the times, I am sure, could run that wild. The problem, then, as I viewed it, wasn't lack of retaliation. Even McNair's parents did not support the idea of retaliatory violence. The problem was the lack of justice in the courts. White-supremacist perpetrators never were convicted, and marches couldn't change the situation or prevent further slaughter. Get-back seemed to be a better approach on this occasion.

Sixth grade is when my teacher noted under "Outstanding Abilities" that I was "an eloquent speaker and very much interested in social studies." Of course, it could hardly have been otherwise given the materials and tools in play. Writing helped me to synthesize notions about current events—civil rights, White backlash, or automation, a hot topic for everyone the way artificial intelligence is now. Conversation shaped what I expressed on the page and, in turn, allowed me to elaborate and judge reception both in and out of school. Developing sharp enough verbal skills was required.

That November, Malcolm X delivered his famous "Message to the Grass Roots," in which he extolled the virtues of Black nationalism and shaped subsequent discussion forums, including barbershops, blocks, and corners. I failed to grasp fully the idea of Black nationalism and perhaps never did. I understood how crucial Black unity could be in civil rights struggles, couldn't conceive of broad social victories without it. However, as to the question of community control, I lacked full awareness of how much we were not in control. As a result, I didn't quite get the program. Over time, it occurred to me that an ideology wasn't the question, disposition was, whether you were Black nationalist enough to carry out a particular action. Temperaments varied in the neighborhood. Approaches were vigorously debated. It was difficult, though, to get around a key Malcolm observation: "Long as the White man sent you to Korea, you bled. He sent you to Germany. You bled. He sent you to the South Pacific to fight the Japanese. You bled. You'll bleed for White people, but when it comes to seeing your own churches being bombed and little Black girls murdered, you haven't got no blood."

The big shock came right after. We were wrapping up the school week when news came that President Kennedy had been shot in Dallas. I didn't envision a motorcade in a congested downtown. Instead, thinking Texas, I conjured up a scene from a western, something like a stagecoach robbery: Kennedy attacked in the desert amid cactus without a lot of people around. I imagined that a marshal and a posse would try to chase down the outlaws. Only when I arrived home after our early dismissal did I get the real picture. Lee Harvey Oswald was in custody, a day away from being the victim in the first murder broadcast live on television. I watched it with my mother.

Some folks in the neighborhood, mostly older, opined that Kennedy had been the best friend of the Negro. They considered him a strong advocate for civil rights even while hamstrung by the Dixiecrat wing of the Democratic Party. Some echoed the "greatest tragedy" rhetoric of *Chicago Defender* publisher John Sengstacke, who offered that comment even after the long string of racist killings covered by his newspaper. I agreed with the idea of tragedy, but not with the idea of a tragedy above all others. My position had support on the block and in the barbershop, but sentiments also squared with Sengstacke's as well, and some veered toward Malcolm X's comment about "chickens coming home to roost," the remark that led to his separation from the Nation of Islam.

The most intriguing local politics to me that school year involved the Princeton Plan, offered as an attempt to end de facto segregation in the city's public schools. If implemented, PS 92, 97 percent Black, and PS 149, 87 percent White, would be "paired." Classes for grades 1 and 2 would be held at 92; students in grades 3–6 would attend 149. In terms of location, you could not have found two better schools, both near

46

the border, to couple. I doubt any student would have had any greater distance to travel than I already did. Most parents in Corona, at least the vocal or activist ones, favored the proposal because they thought it would ensure a more equitable distribution of resources and result in improved education. The logic aligned with that of Reverend Milton Galamison. Heading the Citywide Committee for Integrated Schools, he led a boycott in February in which more than 450,000 students and teachers participated, though none, as far as I recall, from 149.

The Princeton Plan wouldn't affect me personally because my run at 149 was nearing its end. I had desegregated the top class in my grade by myself for five consecutive school terms and was almost through. The uproar in Jackson Heights, much of it represented in the media, is what caught my attention. The *New York Times* reported, for instance, "The yellow traffic line down the middle of Junction Boulevard has become a factor in the greatest domestic controversy this nation has faced since the Civil War. Jackson Heights is 'white.' Corona is 'colored.' Some of the whites refer to the street as 'the dividing line,' and some of the Negroes call it 'the Mason-Dixon Line.'" The lead was hyperbole. In truth, the general opinions about the plan in Jackson Heights and Corona converged to a great degree. Ironically, school leaders in Jackson Heights had proposed the arrangement, and perhaps as much as a third of district residents approved of it. Some helped to form the Citizens Committee for Balanced Schools of Jackson Heights, Corona, and East Elmhurst. But an opposition group, the militant Parents and Taxpayers, vowed to wage a spirited fight against the Princeton Plan. One Jackson Heights resident, quoted anonymously, expressed, "I wish there was some way for everything to be integrated peacefully—you know, there could be one or two colored at first, and maybe more later, and nobody would mind—I know that nobody would mind. It's just the large numbers that I'm afraid of. And that's what everybody else's afraid of, too. Not just in the housing, but in the schools, too." My paranoia kicked in again as I wondered if the putatively liberal Jews whose homes I had visited really were liberal Jews. Or were they akin to the people quoted anonymously? Maybe they were the ones quoted? I contemplated these questions a lot.

Amid the swirl of politics, by far the most popular topic among my classmates, way beyond Birmingham, Malcolm X, Kennedy, and local school factions, was a cultural phenomenon. The Beatles led the so-called British Invasion, which really involved a significant strand of the Black musical influence of Little Richard, Chuck Berry, Bo Diddley, and others returning home. The Beatles had even covered the Miracles' "You Really Got a Hold on Me" and the Isley Brothers' "Twist and Shout," a song first recorded by the Top Notes. John Lennon was no Smokey Robinson or Ronnie Isley or Howie Guyton, but passable. In retrospect, it tickles me that the Beatles arrived in the United States just in time for Black History Week.

I immediately became a fan and was locked in when the Fab Four rode the momentum of their chart-topping "I Want to Hold Your Hand." Along with the rest of the television audience of 75 million, I watched *The Ed Sullivan Show* three consecutive Sundays that February to catch their performances. I was nationalist enough not to spend money on the group; whatever record money I came across went to support Black artists. However, Beatles songs were played on radio so much, especially by Murray the K, that you didn't need their records. They stayed on air and in the air while on their way to locking down the top five spots on the chart at one time. I took a little ribbing on the block, no doubt some of it from undercover Beatles lovers. Notwithstanding, my eventual case for the group has more to do with their songwriting than their recordings. I don't know if they gave as good as they received with respect to Black music, but think of Al Green and Lakeside on "I Want to Hold Your Hand"; Aretha Franklin on "Eleanor Rigby" and "Let It Be"; Stevie Wonder on "We Can Work It Out"; Sarah Vaughan, Ray Charles, Marvin Gaye, Lee Morgan, and En Vogue on "Yesterday"; Otis Redding on "Day Tripper"; Ella Fitzgerald and Stanley Turrentine on "Can't Buy Me Love"; Dionne Warwick on "A Hard Day's Night"; Wes Montgomery and Grant Green on "A Day in the Life"; Wilson Pickett on "Hey Jude"; the Detroit Emeralds on "And I Love Her"; Earth, Wind & Fire on "Got to Get You into My Life"; Tina Turner on "Come Together"; and the cover albums by Count Basie and His Orchestra and George Benson, *Basie's Beatle Bag* and *The Other Side of Abbey Road*, respectively. Moreover, the Beatles wouldn't play Jim Crow, forcing the organizers of the Gator Bowl concert to cave in and permit the audience to be integrated.

Sonny Liston, my original badman—*gorilla monster beast bad for the black image*—refused to be photographed with the Beatles when they visited Miami. He gracelessly referred to them as sissies and held a low

48

opinion of their musicianship, declaring that his dog could play drums better than Ringo Starr. Liston's rejection led to a consolation prize, a photograph session at the 5th Street Gym with Cassius Clay, who was preparing to meet Liston in the ring for the heavyweight title.

Cassius spoiled the following week. I turned twelve on Monday; he beat Liston on Tuesday. Liston was the first of my sports gods to crash to earth. The cry of "fix" resonated in some quarters, folks not comprehending that Liston's challenger was a next-level phenomenon with hands at least as fast as Patterson while being much taller, heavier, stronger, and nimbler of foot. A fix might have been insurance, but Liston didn't have much of a chance—maybe a puncher's chance if the fight had gone past the six rounds it went.

My disappointment didn't linger. Liston personified badness, but Clay personified boldness, even brashness. He unapologetically asserted his Black identity, becoming Muhammad Ali the week after his boxing triumph, although the newspapers insisted on calling him Clay. I morphed into an Ali phase, him becoming more important to me than Liston. My adulation might have developed sooner had I known that Ali had formed a mutual admiration society with Langston Hughes. They met when Ali was in New York for the Doug Jones fight. The budding poet Ali told Hughes that he liked "I, Too, Sing America" and asked for more poems. Hughes gave him several books and later wrote him notes. The two might even have been cousins. Hughes's paternal great-grandfather was Sam Clay, a White man who lived in Kentucky and was a relative of the prominent statesman Henry Clay. Ali's birth name derived from Cassius Marcellus Clay, who was a second cousin to Henry Clay. As far as I know, it has not been determined if there's a biological Hughes-Ali link. Strangely enough, Hughes would be accused of trying to imitate Ali when he wrote rhyming speech for the narrator (Sidney Poitier) of the television special *The Strolling '20s*.

I received all "Excellents" on my final report card except for "Good" in social living. Maybe I finally received "Good" because I joined the Cub Scouts and volunteered to serve as a school crossing guard, sporting with pride my white, plastic safety patrol belt and metal badge. I held down the northeast corner at the intersection of 93rd Street and 34th Avenue for all the little kiddies. I still have my certificate from the Automobile Association of America. Maybe I received credit for having a significant role, the Sergeant of Police, in the sixth-grade production of *The Pirates of Penzance*. I was attentive during rehearsals and led, heaven forbid, "When a Felon's Not Engaged in His Employment," and got the pirates, including Lonnie, to surrender in the name of Queen Victoria. Neither of my parents attended the performance, but some of my classmates' parents commended me for doing a good job. Or maybe I was simply less talkative, more withdrawn that year. That would indicate good deportment.

On the last day of the term, we had a softball game underway. After I had hit a triple, I looked up and saw Lonnie and several other friends, some from Junction Park and PS 92, coming from the direction of right field after climbing through a hole in the fence. I could sense trouble because they hardly bothered with the playground at 149. They proceeded to take over the game, a guy named Bishop seizing the bat from the batter at the plate. When he demanded to be pitched to, the pitcher, Mark Greenberg, refused, causing Bishop to head his way. By that time, Lonnie, my blood brother, was standing over at third base with me and announcing matter-of-factly that the pitcher was about to catch a beatdown. "He should have pitched" is all I would say. Lonnie agreed although he added that, with school concluded, somebody, perhaps everybody on the field except me, needed their ass beat. Bishop never teed off on Mark, just roughly shoved him around to see what would happen. Only Marty Rosenberger seemed unafraid. He appeared ready to run from the near dugout and take up for Mark, who was looking at me as though I could intervene. But this wasn't the third grade, and I would be put in no more trick bags for them.

Bishop pushed Mark to the ground and headed for the terrified shortstop. The other Black kids had fanned out to enact their own scenes of harassment. Possibly looking to do damage, Lonnie headed for the dugout. I pulled ahead of him, flipped Marty to the ground, and pinned him by sitting on his chest, using the dugout fence to brace myself. Lonnie roared with approval, grabbed a bat, and chased everyone else from the dugout. Marty struggled to get loose—"Get off of me, Raymond!"— while I explained that I was keeping him from getting pummeled. He protested that the situation was not fair and that he was unafraid. But I figured I was fair.

None of my playmates put up enough resistance to get hurt. They lost the bat, which Lonnie held up like a torch, and a couple of gloves. "Hey, Keith, we gotta split," Lonnie called over to me. "Come on." I never knew how Marty explained the event. I never knew how any of the boys felt about the beginning of their summer vacation.

8

I hardly knew what to do with myself or even what myself was—certainly a bundle of contradictions if nothing else. I desired mainstream success and had put in the work to be in my mind on track for it. I needed a presentation of self, as the sociologist Erving Goffman would say, that kept me moving in that direction. Or as poet and playwright Useni Eugene Perkins put it, I needed to be a Regular, that is, an accepted member of the streets without having to adhere to all the expectations of the streets. I had to interact with my blood brother Lonnie Blair but be able to resist influences not in my best interest. I had to be one of the fellas and not one of the fellas. That was no easy trick and could only be managed with delicate dodging. However, no matter the degree of nimbleness, the interplay among mainstream culture, school culture, and home culture, including the languages associated with each, inevitably produced ambivalence.

When I read Herbert Kohl's *36 Children*, his account of teaching sixth grade in Harlem in 1962 and 1963, I was particularly interested in the student named Grace, who was about my age. She had been Kohl's most academically advanced student, had made a special progress class, as I had done, and eventually received a scholarship to a prep school in New England. By analyzing letters Grace wrote to him, Kohl concluded that Grace became alienated from Harlem even though she was "too poor and too much of a special case" to be fully part of the prep school world. He wondered if her alienation would render her asunder or lead to a productive synthesis. He asked, in other words, if she could solve problems created by grown-ups.

Shortly after I finished PS 149, I was stunned to see Mrs. Goldberg in the A&P on 108th Street and Northern Boulevard, deep into Corona. She was the mother of Stephen Goldberg, a former classmate. I had visited her home several times and was always treated well. I couldn't fathom why she would be in that supermarket and not at one down in Jackson

Heights. Because I spotted her before she saw me, I was able to alter my course and avoid being seen. I didn't plan my reaction. It seems I should have said hello. But I didn't.

President Johnson forced the Civil Rights Act through Congress to guarantee, supposedly, the desegregation of public facilities and the widespread implementation of affirmative action. Naturally, we figured the jury remained out on what those papers would solve, given that voting rights had not been addressed and Freedom Summer had begun in tragedy with the murder in Mississippi of voting-rights activists James Chaney, Andrew Goodman, and Michael Schwerner. Tragedy in the North unfolded after an incident involving a mean building superintendent water hosing Black students who sat on stoops while in the area to attend summer school. The super allegedly vowed to wash niggers clean. As the episode played out, police officer Thomas Gilligan shot and killed James Powell, a fifteen-year-old student from the Bronx, who stood five-six and weighed about 120 pounds. According to Gilligan, Powell wielded a knife, although none was recovered at the scene that day. The shooting set off several days of rioting in Harlem and other parts of the city, most notably the Bedford-Stuyvesant section of Brooklyn. President Johnson suggested that Communists had instigated the riots and dispatched the FBI to investigate. Some people in Harlem shouted down Bayard Rustin and his pleas for nonviolence. They called for Malcolm X. How much rage was silent and swallowed could not be gauged.

The childhood part of me longed to attend the World's Fair, which had opened with controversy that April practically in our backyard. While those who ran New York City wished to display opulence and innovation, members of the Brooklyn and Bronx chapters of CORE wanted to protest matters such as job discrimination, deteriorating housing, poor schools, and police brutality. They issued a statement: "While millions of dollars are being spent on the World's Fair, thousands of Black & Puerto Rican people are suffering."

They planned a stall-in, an idea first articulated by journalist Louis Lomax. He proposed that hundreds of drivers purposely run out of gas or otherwise stop on the highways leading to the fairgrounds, creating a massive traffic jam and thus disrupting the opening because tens of thousands would be unable to get there. These were "our" highways, the Grand Central Parkway bordering Corona, leading into the Van

Wyck Expressway and the Interboro Parkway a few miles away, with the Brooklyn-Queens Expressway nearby in the other direction. This promised to be quite a spectacle if it came off and a lot of extra excitement for us. However, a court injunction against Brooklyn CORE, heavy police presence on all highways into Queens, and rainy, chilly weather combined to render the stall-in almost nil, although the prospect of the civil disobedience action severely diminished attendance at the fair. Several hundred college students did manage to heckle President Johnson during his keynote address at the U.S. Federal Pavilion, shouting over him and holding up signs. Read one: "A World's Fair Is a Luxury but a Fair World Is a Necessity."

We kids were within walking distance of the phenomenal exposition to which people eventually streamed from all over the world. We went often, finding the free route, a compromised fence next to the tracks for the Long Island Railroad, that became an open secret, and experienced every single exhibit, including the monorail, the Unisphere, the Pepsi Tour of the Globe, and the display of thermonuclear fusion at the General Electric Pavilion. I kept returning to the latter, receiving a thrill each time they heated the deuterium chamber to 20 million degrees, or so they said, to fill the exhibit hall with the thunder-and-lightning effect. And I was awed by the display of rockets, one so massive it couldn't be assembled fully for show. I wondered if the Russians could match that, but there was no exhibit from them because the parties involved in the negotiations failed to reach an agreement. In any case, the future loomed as wonderful, or at least as much more convenient. General Motors, Chrysler, and American Telephone and Telegraph would ensure it. We would all have telephones with video screens and flying cars like George Jetson in the cartoon.

Late one morning, after roaming about the fairgrounds, Wallace Jones and I, tired and hungry, headed for the block. Wallace had become as close to me as had Lonnie Blair, whom I saw less of as time went by. He was the younger of two brothers. I became an honorary Jones boy because I was at their dinner table so often. As we stepped out onto Roosevelt Avenue with the Number 7 train roaring by overhead, we looked across at deserted Shea Stadium, the new home of the New York Mets. It opened the week before the fair. The Braves, Dodgers, and Giants were due in soon, and I looked forward to seeing Hank Aaron, the

Davis boys—Tommy and Willie—Maury Wills, and the still-great Willie Mays. We also knew how to sneak into the stadium.

When two redheaded White boys about our size came cycling along Roosevelt toward Flushing on two gold-colored ten-speeds and Wallace suggested that we scare them, I had no objection, unaware that Wallace, known to be impulsive, had decided to take one of the bikes. The boy tried to steer around us but was knocked off balance when Wallace punched him in the head. The boy had heart, though. He dismounted and started mixing it up until Wallace dropped him with a kick to the groin. The move was from a type of kick boxing we called stato. Wallace snatched up the bike and began his getaway. Meanwhile, I had control of the other bike because the rider had hopped off to see about his companion, whom I assumed to be his brother. A driver coming along Roosevelt saw what was happening and tried to cut Wallace off with his car but missed. He leaped from the car brandishing a club, thinking he was close enough to catch Wallace on foot. No chance. By the time he hurled the club at Wallace, missing, I had begun pedaling hard on the other bike. No way I could handle that man. Fearful and exhilarated, Wallace and I zigzagged, turning at every corner.

In short order we led a bike-stealing craze. We doubled up on bikes we already had and went scouting in White neighborhoods. When we discovered a target, the one who had to get the bike was dropped off to snip the chain, raid the yard, throw the blow, or do whatever else was necessary. There was no turning back. You either stole the bike or walked home. Maybe take a bus if you had the fare. Sometimes we rode single and traded in bikes for ones we thought were better. It goes without saying that no virtue existed in this behavior. This was not hard-luck Antonio Ricci.

I couldn't keep any of the bikes at my home. I left mine with friends who weren't questioned the way I would have been. We were in backyards filing off serial numbers, switching parts, and spray-painting frames. After reports flooded into local precincts, mainly the 109th, 110th, and 114th, the *Long Island Press* ran a story about a suspected organized ring. We laughed about that one. We didn't imagine ourselves as being organized and certainly didn't net any money. In fact, although a few refashioned two-wheelers were sold, we destroyed just as many. Down at Giant Rock, a thousand-ton boulder in a wooded lot off Ditmars Boulevard, we would line bikes up against the base, gather numerous stones, and, from a distance we agreed would establish who among us was the best marksman, we damaged as many spokes as we could. Several bikes were disabled completely and left behind.

Wallace was almost nabbed in Jackson Heights, barely made it back before a squad car, with a White boy in the back seat, circled the block a few times. That was signal enough to me to chill on those adventures for a spell. Plenty other action awaited anyway. We would go over to Flushing Bay, what we called, simply, the Bay. It didn't smell as much when the tide was in, but we hung out there either way. We might try to catch eels, stone rats, or skip pebbles across the water. We would watch the airplanes take off and land at LaGuardia at the western end of the bay. At the eastern end sat the marina, where, before the barbed-wire fence was erected, we would sneak onto the anchored boats to explore that lifestyle and relax, listening to the waves ripple and dash up against the sides. My group never vandalized boats, but somebody did. That's what brought the fence.

The Bay was also home to a lovers' lane. You could find a used condom, nudge it onto the edge of a stick, and chase your friends with it. I'm sure I ran some of my fastest sprints to avoid being tagged. Sex, naturally, was always on the horizon, usually sublimated, at least back on the block, into games. We played Spin the Bottle or a little game called Truth? Dare? Consequences? Promise? or Repeat? Most of us chose the Dare option. We wanted to be dared to kiss so-and-so for a specified count. That's how some of us obtained our first tight embraces and soulful kisses—in other words, how we prepped for "macking out." White folks were "making out," so a different linguistic flair is what we inherited. A lot of behind-the-scenes daring and macking out went on, but I couldn't always be sure that the reports I heard were true.

There were more things to squeeze into summer. You will never convince Pat that she and I were not the supreme bottle-hunting team in the neighborhood. We were out early in the morning scouring for bottles to redeem. This was quite a feat for a notoriously late sleeper like my sister. The streets and vacant lots yielded a fair amount, but the key was to go door-to-door over in East Elmhurst. We found out that some residents ordered big sodas by the crate and stacked empty bottles in their basements. The big bottles brought you five cents as opposed to two cents for the small ones. I would ring the bell and adorable Pat would take the lead and make the inquiry when someone answered. One day we hit the mother lode. Despite several trips, we couldn't clear out the basement in one morning. However, the woman who let us in promised to hold the rest until we could get to them. We made enough that day to go to Astoria Pool, a popular destination even though I never learned to swim. Splashing in shallow water to beat the heat was enough for me. Once Pat and I couldn't resist spending all our money on refreshments. We lacked the discipline to put the bus fare aside and had to walk the four miles home and become hungry all over again. I don't know what food awaited us that day, but a mayonnaise sandwich and sugar water would not have been an unusual solution for me.

Even more things to squeeze in. I now lived four blocks from Louis Armstrong, who could have lived a lot of other places—and his wife wanted him to—but chose to remain in Corona, where he had maintained a residence for more than twenty years. I was oblivious to the scope of his contribution to jazz and to the accusations of selling out and Uncle Tomism. I did know that with his gravelly voice and recording of "Hello, Dolly" he surprisingly knocked the Beatles from the top of the chart. I aimed to attend one of his cookouts for kids that I heard about. In the meantime, more of the World's Fair. Games at Shea Stadium. My mother (paying a dollar and thirty cents for me, which I knew was unnecessary) took us to watch the Mets play the Dodgers, the reigning World Series champions. Junior Gilliam was still a favorite of hers based on his days at Ebbets Field. I was more concerned with the contemporary. *When dust settled near the base / Maury Wills again was safe.*

We tracked the march of the Yankees to another pennant, this time led by rookie manager Yogi Berra. The Phillies under Gene Mauch blew it in the National League by losing ten in a row. We had marbles championships to contend for, games of jacks to win. We had to master spinning tops, build go-carts, try our hand at raising pigeons. Throw in skelly, skates, boxing gloves, limbo sticks, and jump rope. And always the music. Dance all over the street, just as Martha and the Vandellas said, and there were so many steps to learn along the way to junior high school.

9

PS 149 tempted me because of the protests. White parents brought dozens of first and second graders to the school when those students had been assigned to PS 92 because of pairing. Mr. Price couldn't stop them from occupying classrooms. The parents repeated the sit-in a second day with news crews all around. Mr. Price held a press conference in his office. I hated to miss it. My younger sisters were in the grades affected by the desegregation plan, but they had been sent to PS 14 on Otis Avenue.

I also had to get settled in school. Although I had qualified for a special progress class, officials ticketed me for Junior High School 16, which didn't offer such a class. Joining a large group of students who had attended PS 92, the most African American schoolmates I had since Harlem, I was expected to trek across Roosevelt Avenue into Corona Heights. I hoped my nerves were ready on all fronts. The school did have Artie the Cop on hand, a sign of expected clashes that could come from any angle.

Auntie took away one worry, my wardrobe. Intent on helping her sister and seeing her nephew begin the term in fashion—an increasingly important concern for me after a couple of episodes of flapping soles and cardboard inserts—she took me on a shopping trip in the Bronx, where she lived. We started at Alexander's on 3rd Avenue, garnering pants, dress shirts, socks, underwear, and handkerchiefs. Then we got several pairs of shoes, including black ripple-soles and brown suede crepe soles. Sartorially, I could not have been more prepared.

My mother appreciated the help but wasn't going for the school program. She wanted me in a special progress class and proceeded to the Board of Education headquarters on Livingston Street in downtown Brooklyn to make sure it happened. She preferred getting me into JHS 145 in Jackson Heights, which Barbara and most former 149 students, including Lonnie Blair, attended. That wasn't allowed because the board determined that I was out of the zone, although I shared the same address with my sister. The board reasoned that Barbara had been designated for assignment before we moved from 96th Street. The fact that I had attended 149 for the sixth grade, seemingly from out of the zone, given that I didn't know anyone else who lived that far east in Corona who went to the school, didn't matter. The compromise reached was that I would enroll at JHS 73, William Cowper Junior High School, way over in Maspeth. I would be among the early waves of African American students sent to that school and, through the same zoning maneuver, so was the other half of the new dynamic duo, Wallace Jones.

I didn't know of my mother's actions during those first days at JHS 16. After a couple of days, I grew more comfortable in the yard. Schoolwork was no problem. I was sitting in Mr. Frazier's class when a monitor entered with a note summoning me to the principal's office. That's when I found out about the transfer. When I arrived at Cowper, the two-year special progress class, number 7-19—compressing the seventh and eighth grades into one academic term—was reportedly full and I was assigned to a three-year class, 7-17. My mother had an urge to protest this move also, but then she decided that the three-year program wouldn't be so bad after all. Not liking the pressure, Barbara had asked out of the two-year class at 145.

The trip to JHS 73 could be involved and usually took at least an hour. You could take a bus to Flushing to link up with the first stop of the Number 58 bus and start a long, winding path to Maspeth. This route took you down Corona Avenue past Newtown High School, past Broadway, and along Grand Avenue. You always had a seat, but you had to deal with the Newtown crowd. The racial mix could be volatile in 1964. Or you had different ways to bypass Newtown, get to the subway stop at Broadway and Queens Boulevard, and pick up the 58 there. No matter how you went, you were on the bus long enough to encounter White students going to Grover Cleveland High School in neighboring Ridgewood. That could be another issue.

A grade of 65 was generally the minimum passing mark in school, but our minimum standard in special progress was 85. Marks below that on our report card were circled with red ink as a reminder that they were below expectation. Too many red circles could get you dismissed. I wasn't worried because I felt that I could achieve whatever I wanted. My mother had trained me to *handle* things, to be excellent beyond any distraction.

I had a couple of African American classmates, the first, other than the ones at JHS 16, who sat in a classroom with me since the first grade.

David Taylor from East Elmhurst, down on the other side of the baseball field, was an affable student. I don't recall what he said about his elementary school experience or where he attended. I do remember that he dressed well, even had a few knit shirts that made me a little envious, and he was academically smart. We formed a friendship almost immediately. We rounded on the White classmates who sported tight pants, Beatles boots, Nehru shirts, and greased hair. Or we noted the plain, bargain-store quality of the clothes that some of our other classmates wore. David and I didn't realize that their parents were already saving for college tuition.

I began to slide after only a few weeks. I couldn't focus on schoolwork, wouldn't do my homework thoroughly—if at all. Only math proved motivating, the puzzles of algebra as presented by Mrs. Friedman. She said that with my aptitude I should become an accountant. Other classes were boring by comparison. I didn't care much about science experiments or Spanish. I lacked interest in grammar lessons and classroom social studies.

At least a bright spot outside class was that conservative hawk Barry Goldwater got stomped in the presidential election. The infamous daisy commercial portraying a nuclear explosion and mushroom clouds crippled his campaign. He only carried his home state of Arizona and, because he was a states' rights advocate, which was music to the ears of Dixiecrats, the Deep South—Georgia, Alabama, Mississippi, Louisiana, and South Carolina.

A different danger was near, one that I could feel but not define. I couldn't get the tangled web of personality and environment to unravel. One thing was clear, however. I mightily resisted the physical control mechanisms of school. The dress code was restrictive; ties were required every day. We were ordered never to cross the thick red line to reach a classroom but to instead walk to the end of the hall before cutting to the other side. We were instructed to use the up staircase for going up, the down staircase for going down. A book was already out about how stupid that regulation was. Line up in the yard, obedient like the kids I used to guide at the intersection. We were not supposed to leave the building during lunch period. This regimentation had no redeeming value I could see, especially given that I was often left to babysit a six-year-old at home. Once I had to go to the store on the Boulevard for my mother and took Frances along. She cried when I wouldn't buy her the candy she wanted.

60

I didn't have any money on me. My solution—executive decision—was to spend our mother's change. Baby sister cries, she gets what she wants. Our mother would just have to understand, which she did.

So I viewed these school rules as simply something to break, a decision that introduced me to a variety of disciplinary measures. For example, because I hardly ever wore a tie, I had to fold a sheet of loose leaf twice over lengthwise, print the word "tie" on it, poke a hole in it, and fasten that paper tie to a button on my shirt. I always had at least one button available because collarless shirts were banned. David had to wear a tie with some of the knit shirts he had. Some guys used more paper on ties than on homework. I wasn't quite that bad. I owned ties but just had trouble getting with the program.

On my report card, my marks hovered in the 80s with the exceptions of a 92 in math and a 95 in gym. That I had to improve was simple enough to see. I needed to be more diligent with homework. But Wallace was puzzled because with his collection of 65s, which was fine by him, he didn't understand the code of special progress. Why would a teacher draw a red circle around an 80? It seemed too much to explain that I should have been receiving at least 90 in every subject. My mother was confused also and squinted at each grade that appeared peculiar to her. She did sign the card but stated flatly, "You can do better." That was indisputable.

One morning in late November, I exited the bakery across Grand Avenue after buying some beloved crumb buns. These were to be hidden in my desk and sneakily munched on during early classes, another prohibited activity. I would be finished by lunch period. Wallace ran over from the soda shop, dodging cars along the way, with news fresh off the grapevine. There was a hooky party and a good chance, he advised, to get my thing wet. Couldn't play games on the block forever. Ditching school, we pulled our bus passes back out, doubled back to Corona, and went to Benjamin's house. Apparently, too many people had heard about this party. It wasn't anywhere near latter-day flash-mob level, but more than Benjamin wanted to be bothered with. He especially didn't want unattached guys around. Girls brought other girls, a move considered okay. Wallace knew one of them. I received a pass because Benjamin, a high schooler, was tight with Rob Jones, and, for many purposes, I was another Jones boy, a well-dressed one. That earned me a trey bag.

As the gathering settled, music spun out from the hi-fi, artists such as Smokey Robinson and Little Anthony. The aroma of pancakes and marijuana began to fill the air. Bacon shriveling, natures expanding. Sugar passed with sugar. Lemons squeezed with girls. The most basic of dances all around me. Self-conscious, I went over by the hi-fi and managed to assume disc jockey duties.

People drifted about the house, and I eventually found myself alone in the living room with two beautiful girls, Chrystal and Helen. Both had me by a couple years. When, in response to my query, they said they smoked herb, I pulled the reefer and the Bambu rolling paper from my pocket. I asked if they could roll, and they both said they rolled well. Of course, I didn't because I had never tried.

My first toke jacked me up. I inhaled too much and coughed violently. I alibied that I had a cold and swore to myself that I would be smoother. I got my technique together, a much softer draw. Instead of the floating sensation I expected based on things I had heard, I just felt giddy and on the verge of blowing my cool. However, I held it together. The talk was light: identification of common acquaintances, the merits and demerits of our respective schools, opinions on popular songs and singers, what records to play next. Then I really did blow my cool. When Helen left to go to the store, I figured that was the set-up. I slid next to Chrystal on the couch for the mack out and said, "So come on." I told her she knew the scoop. She pushed me away and spoke defiantly: "What's wrong with you, boy? Ain't no scoop here. What makes you think I like you anyway?" She wanted to know with whom I had been trading stories. I finally convinced her that it was nobody. Chrystal never talked to me again. I mean over years and years she didn't. If she saw me approaching and had time, she would cross the street. I couldn't think of anything to say. I had a catalogue but no rap, no eloquence in that domain.

I once was brought to this girl's house by a friend of mine named Kevin Roots. I had been talking about her, so he decided to let her know. We rode over on bicycles. He tapped on her window. When she opened it, he greeted her and rode away. I sat on my bike practically speechless for fifteen minutes or so before being dismissed. It looked like some girl would have to run up on me one day and utter something tantamount to "So come on."

Around Christmas, I was sitting in Auntie's kitchen in the Bronx reading a magazine article about Martin Luther King Jr., who that month became the youngest person ever to receive the Nobel Peace Prize. Auntie said the award just went to show that King was a great leader. I was more concerned with his fame than with his politics, though I admired him the right way for her. I said he wasn't loquacious just for show. He was trying to get things done. Auntie asked where I got the word *loquacious*. She said I had a good head for the books and could be like King, be the best, if I wanted to. She admonished me to follow the books because they would take me places, and she gently warned me not to be a follower or get caught up in the wrong crowd. The sisters had been talking. Auntie later suggested that I come live with her, an idea my mother adamantly rejected.

In February Malcolm fell to assassins. I hadn't figured it to go that way. When they firebombed his home, Wallace and I walked over, eleven blocks away, to survey the damage. Neither Malcolm nor his family was around. Nor were reporters any longer. Police were still on the scene in the freezing cold, and a few passersby paused, as we did, to gaze at the broken windows and the charred rubble in the driveway and get a peek at the scorched living room. I saw the bombing as simply a scare tactic because I thought assassins operated with more precision.

Malcolm's death walloped me. The neighborhood reaction was more reserved, the expressions of grief more muted than was the case with President Kennedy. However, lively debate concerning the reason for the assassination unfolded in barbershops I visited in Harlem and Queens. I couldn't get a firm read. Some blamed Communists, some the CIA. Still others placed the blame on dope dealers who were said to resent efforts by Malcolm to fight drug trafficking in Harlem. Of course, a faction argued that the Muslims were responsible. A fire was started at the mosque uptown on 116th Street. By Monday morning, a police patrol guarded Temple 7B on Northern Boulevard, one block from my home. When we came out to go to school, officers were lined up along Northern Boulevard and on 105th Street, heading toward 32nd Avenue. Watching this is how I entered my teenage years. Two weeks later came the reports of Bloody Sunday in Selma, Alabama, where state and county police attacked peaceful protesters on the Edmund Pettus Bridge and injured dozens, including, most infamously, Amelia Boynton Robinson and John Lewis.

10

Back in school I was mired in mediocrity, which is what 80s and 85s in SP amounted to, fortunate not to be doing worse. Academically, I limped to the finish line of the school term. However, because I wasn't bounced from the program as a couple other students were, I would have a chance to improve after an off year and secure redemption.

That summer we repeated much of the routine from the year before. The new wrinkles were that we added Colt .45 malt liquor, Bacardi rum, and Bali Hai wine (never much of those things for me), and a little marijuana. One of my highlights, however, was a perfectly sober and sobering moment. It happened on what couldn't have been a calmer Saturday afternoon. An uncontroversial stickball game unfolded, good competition without arguments. Right in the middle of it I was summoned home to mop the kitchen floor. Nothing strange about the request except that it was bad timing for my serenity. Upset, I became irrational. Instead of following my norm and discharging the task promptly, I sulked and procrastinated, aggravating my mother. She placidly ordered me to stop fooling around—pussyfooting, as she called it—and do what I had been told. That was reasonable. My response was not. I replied that I would do it when I was ready. She couldn't believe what I said, questioning me until I repeated it deliberately and forcefully. She trembled with anger, and I knew she would be at her most intimidating, wielding a severed ironing cord.

The pain flamed through my T-shirt like fire, singeing my back and spreading to my arms. I clenched my fists as tightly as I could and refused to utter even a whimper. She couldn't break me. When she went to lash at my arms, now folded against my chest, our eyes locked fiercely. Whatever she saw in mine made her lose steam. She hit me a few harmless licks and stormed off to her bedroom, slamming the door behind her.

I retreated to the bathroom, latched the door behind me, and leaned back against it. Sore, but wanting to howl with joy. I had achieved a victory so immense and dangerous it couldn't all sink in just then. I moved to the mirror and proudly inspected my welts. I checked my eyes, stretched my face, squinted, tried all the variations of my Sonny Liston glare. But I didn't see anything in the mirror that I imagined would startle or frighten or defeat anybody. I couldn't linger on speculation, however. I had a floor to mop and was determined to do an excellent job. Why make my stand on that day and at that time? I doubt I'll ever obtain a precise answer.

That was the outstanding event for me until a White highway patrolman stopped motorist Marquette Frye on suspicion of drunken driving. Frye apparently resisted and was met with overwhelming force. Amid a heightened police presence and protests from community observers, both Marquette and his brother Ronald Frye, who accompanied him, were beaten and arrested. Their mother, Rena, who had arrived on the scene, was arrested as well. With long-term exploitation, excessive police force, and simmering resentment coalescing, the Watts district and much of Black Los Angeles exploded. Snipers and blazes and twenty thousand government troops and looting and machine guns and tear gas and bayonets and curfews. Thirty-four dead. Over one thousand injured. Over three thousand arrested. This was the most shocking incident I had seen on television yet, beyond Harlem and the murder of Oswald. It was exactly what I didn't need.

President Johnson denounced Black rioters, lumping them with the Ku Klux Klan as destroyers of the country. But Johnson would never send twenty thousand troops to attack the Klan. Even on occasions when he might restrain them, you would not see three thousand Klansmen arrested.

My decline in school continued. My average in major subjects fell from 84 to 77, mostly because of a 65 in Spanish. Foreign languages require real study. I had a feeling that my time in SP was nearly concluded because I failed to meet the bar of responsibility. I surmise that scoring well on standardized tests such as the Iowa Tests of Educational Development kept me in.

Amid all this, English became my favorite class. I appreciated how Mrs. Applebaum challenged us. A model of confidence and style, she claimed to be totally unimpressed with how intelligent we were alleged to be. She told us, in fact, that we were vastly overrated. As evidence, she brought in an article from the *New York Times* about African American students in Harlem who were doing amazing things academically. She praised them over us.

Mrs. Applebaum had me on the ball for a while, given that she threw down the gauntlet. Although I didn't produce all she thought I should have, I absorbed plenty. From her I gained my greatest understanding of the short story in general and of Poe's "unity of effect" via his cold-blooded "The Cask of Amontillado." Fortunato surely messed with the wrong dude. O. Henry's "The Gift of the Magi" fascinated me. It was generally viewed in class as a tale of great love and selflessness, but my mother often stated that love is an understanding between two fools. Mrs. Applebaum laughed at this and suggested that both my mother and I might make good literary critics. I had to inform my teacher that Sydney Carton was kind of a fool, too, in *The Tale of Two Cities*, but you couldn't argue with his heart or the best closing lines in literature: "It is a far, far better thing . . ."

Mrs. Applebaum persuaded me to enter the oral recitation contest. As part of a group effort, I had read parts of Alfred Noyes's "The High-wayman" compellingly in class, and she thought I would do well. We even arranged after-school practice sessions to get the whole lyrically enchanting poem down pat. When I went to register, I was told that the selection had to be by an American author. I instantly decided not to participate. After all, our school was named after a British poet. Why were we privileging Americans? "The Highwayman" was good enough for me. Even Cowper's "The Negro's Complaint" would have been suitable. At any rate, after Mrs. Applebaum persuaded me to perform, and I couldn't decide on a Langston Hughes poem, we settled on some long patriotic poem by William Cullen Bryant, probably "America" (can't remember), and I was totally outclassed. Mrs. Applebaum congratulated me on my effort nonetheless. Looking back, I wish I had known about James Weldon Johnson and Margaret Walker.

Russia didn't worry students anymore, partly because it couldn't win in the movies against James Bond. We had a scare, though, with the Great Northeast Blackout. My family had moved next door to the upstairs apartment. Our landlord lived in the apartment under us, and that's where I spent most of the night talking with Mr. Bob and wondering when power would be restored. It's also where I spent time during the mass transportation strike that kicked off the new year. Word on the streets was that when Wagner left office, every union would strike because underhanded Wagner deals would no longer be in play. As soon as Mayor Lindsay was sworn in, Mike Quill led the Transport Workers Union in a wildcat action that shut down the subway system. The Amalgamated Transit Union joined in, which meant most buses were out of service. All this added up to no school for a few days.

I read some of the news coverage to Mr. Bob. He used to pretend to be literate, often sending me to the store for a newspaper. After he had listened to a ballgame or the news on the radio, he would open the paper and begin a discussion as though he were referencing an article. One day he had the paper opened to pages with no pictures. He held the pages upside down!

To the melody of "Don't Mess with Bill," a Marvelettes tune that had been released recently, some of us young folks sang, "Don't Mess with Quill. No, no, no, no." Quill was jailed with several others for breaking a court injunction. In his Irish brogue, he declared that the judge could "drop dead in his black robes." He might have wanted to take back those words. Quill himself suffered a heart attack and didn't make it to the end of January, although the strike could be considered a success.

Speaking of singing, it's central to my memories of JHS 73. During assembly, we performed choral singing of "Frère Jacques." Sections of the auditorium started at different times. It wasn't much musical fun, singing a nursery rhyme with words I didn't know the meaning of, but as a concentration exercise it had value. If everyone stayed on verse, we would all finish at the same intervals at which we began. The most exciting assembly featured Mickey and his partners—I think they were all ninth graders—doo-wopping Don and Juan's 1962 hit "What's Your Name?" They had me leaning toward songwriting, but one line is all I could get. Whenever I tried, I'd write, "Have you ever seen a girl go by?" That's my one line forever. I'm destined never to be a Claude (Juan) Johnson. The only consolation is that, thinking about song lyrics, I was in the vicinity of poetry again.

Michael Saunders represented Frank Sinatra. He would tell me to expand my taste and then, while seated behind me, he would lean over and whisper a rendition of "I Believe in You." Cool clear eyes and seek wisdom and truth? I could go for that. Count Basie's Orchestra backed

Sinatra; Quincy Jones did the charts. Nothing not to like. You might be familiar with Michael as Mike Saunders, athletic trainer for the New York Knicks for twenty-seven years. He was solid in junior high school. He had heart and always stood up for himself.

I looked for the so-called normal paths. Following my stint with the Cub Scouts, I joined the Boy Scouts at St. Gabriel's. While not a scout for long, I did hang around long enough to obtain a sleeping bag and mess kit and go on a weekend bus trip to Alpine Scout Camp, located in the Palisades over in New Jersey. My father funded my participation and went with us. We had our first extended visit in years in a lean-to out in the woods. And it was strange under the stars. Twinkle, twinkle, all that possibility floating in the nighttime sky.

I played Little League baseball with the Space Angels, proudly sporting the red and white and holding down either second base or third. Mr. Ray, who had a cleaning establishment on Northern Boulevard, sponsored us but hardly ever talked baseball with me, preferring to find out how I was doing overall. Our coach, Mr. Anderson, gave me my first and only pair of baseball shoes. I missed a game because I forgot my cap at home. I told Mr. Anderson that it was only a cap. He said if I didn't come dressed to play, I didn't play. I always played after that. Our football team, on which I played with schoolmates such as Ronald Gray and Anthony Merkerson, was centered at PS 143, where there was a grass field. We were coached by the amazing athlete Embra Sease and used to go to his house to watch film of our games. I'm on camera on a blitz, clean shot at the running back, and getting, at about five foot four, run over. I'm also on camera with an interception and gaining good yardage while carrying the ball, Jim Brown style, like it was a loaf of bread.

I had the neighborhood covered. I'd go to the night center at PS 127 and win a foul-shooting contest over there. After most sessions at the night center, I'd stop by Cunningham's on Astoria Boulevard for burgers, two for a quarter. Around that time, Manuel Peters got me into cars. Although a good athlete, he was more of a karate guy than a ballplayer and didn't always want to hang around the night center the whole time. He proposed that we go driving, an idea that seemed weird to me because we were fourteen, had no car, and didn't know how to drive anyway. However, my assumption proved to be incorrect. Manuel had been stealing cars and had one stashed nearby. With Manuel behind the wheel and seated on a phone book to give him a good enough view, we drove over to Ditmars Boulevard, which turned out to be a training course. We went along Ditmars, cut over to Astoria Boulevard, and worked our way back around to Ditmars. Manuel drove a few of these laps before turning over the wheel and phone book to me. The steering kicked in almost right away. Straight along Ditmars was no problem. I needed to improve my jerky acceleration, hard braking, and wide turns.

Manuel showed Wallace, who was uncharacteristically reluctant, and me. Today it would be a TikTok challenge. If someone forgot keys, that was straightforward but infrequent. We mostly searched for cars with an ignition knob, a feature on several General Motors models back then. The settings were "On," "Off," and "Lock," and drivers too often settled for "Off." If we spotted that, the next task was to get inside. Sometimes that was too simple because the door was unlocked. Having a door key made things almost as easy. GM didn't cut a lot of different door keys, or maybe it's that the keys weren't differentiated enough. If you had a key, the chances were that if you tried to open other cars with it, you would hit within six or seven tries. Lean on the car with your back against it trying to look innocent while testing the lock. Without a key, you might slip in a hanger to raise the door lock knob. Get in, turn "Off" to "On," and let the joyride begin.

We became good drivers and became absurd again. That year you could catch a school bus to JHS 73, the first pickup being at 108th Street and Northern Boulevard, catty-corner from the A&P. One day I got Wallace to agree that rather than take the bus we would follow it in the car we had stashed. We retrieved it from a couple of blocks away on Couch Street, waited for the bus to load, and followed it from Corona down into Elmhurst and on to Maspeth. Taking turns driving with Wallace, I was jittery all the way. This was morning traffic, horns honking in broad daylight. A patrol car here and there. We were all the way on the other side of wrong and still sitting on phone books. Students on the bus, our friends, crowded at the rear window to observe our progress. They were rowdy, but the bus was always that way. Apparently, the bus driver wasn't tipped off. We arrived at school safely, adjectivally criminal but not in our minds the noun.

II

After some minor roughhousing in the hall, Jay Hayes and I sat in Miss Redd's office. She gave us a homework assignment to write the Gettysburg Address five times. I had no problem. Jay told Miss Redd to suck his dick. She promptly expelled him from JHS 73 and sent him on his way to 600 school, a place for students who needed "adjustment." I had known him for a few years and would continue to see him around the neighborhood. We could connect on something other than disparaging a dean or guidance counselor to her face.

Eventually, Miss Redd would talk to me about wasting good potential and ask why I associated with Jay, Wallace, and others of that ilk. I was an SP student, albeit a sinking one likely headed for juvie. She asked if I thought therapy could help me. Would I be afraid if she could arrange it? Of course, my mother would have to approve. I was unnerved but knew right away that I wasn't seeing no shrink if the matter hinged on my mother's consent. In truth, though, Miss Redd's shrink talk lingered with me, caused me to ponder how much control I had over my own life, whether I was a player or getting played.

After mulling over the proper rhetorical approach, I decided to present Miss Redd's idea as a joke. *Mother dear, the school said I should see a therapist, ha, ha, ha.* The answer was not a surprise: *Nothing wrong with you, boy. Just handle everything the right way.* Her response wasn't merely dismissive, however. In the ensuing days, she prepped me more for life. Observing that I was getting bigger, closing in on her five-six in height, she conceded that she couldn't beat me into doing right. She said I, and Wallace as well, had to be careful in the streets. She didn't trust anyone out there to have our best interest at heart the way she and his parents did. She reminded me of the time I was with a group of boys one Saturday as we looked down upon a man we knew, a notorious figure, sleeping on a lawn chair in his backyard. From our perch, someone decided that we should see who had the best aim and could hit this guy with a pebble.

70

None of the others were able to hit the mark; I figured out too late they were missing on purpose. Ridiculing their lack of skill, I popped him in the chest on my first throw, startling him awake while we burst out in laughter and scattered. I ran straight home. He immediately started tracking us down one by one and discovered that all fingers except Wallace's pointed to me. When he came to our apartment, my mother, while I stood behind her, thanked him for the information and assured him that she would take care of the situation. It was perfect sermon material for her as she stressed the idea of doing right and reading those in my circle. It was the same message, by the way, that my target had for me when he saw me around. Of course, he couldn't ensure a good outcome, no more than my mother could. But it never hurt to hear a positive spin.

My mother also would remind me on occasion of the time she pulled me from a police car around the corner on 105th Street. There had been a running feud between Mr. Watson and some of the guys on the block. I think it had to do with them playing handball against a side of his house and disturbing his peace. It was reasonable to ask them to stop, but they never would, and Mr. Watson called the police. Nothing of consequence happened until the guys chose to give Mr. Watson another reason to call the cops when they doused his car with yellow paint. I wasn't sure who did it, but neither could the police have been, which is what I tried to explain to them after they had placed two of my friends under arrest. My trial-lawyer antics got me tossed into the squad car as well. I got a window seat, quite visible to my mother as she happened to approach on her way up the block. She firmly ordered me to get out and talked to an officer. He agreed to let me go because, as he explained, they were going to take me in only to teach me a lesson about running my mouth.

Her favorite story/lesson also involved the police. She received a call that I was snooping around a parking lot near the stadium. The police did not allege that I'd committed any crime, only that I was acting suspiciously. They told her that they were sending me home. As my mother hung up the receiver, I walked through the door with Wallace. Without teleportation, I couldn't be the person that had been detained. I never found out who had used my name and number, but he was no friend. It didn't matter to my mother; her point had been proven. She hoped that I remained attentive as she continued to explain right from wrong. She said she would always support me when I was in the right and sometimes even in the wrong if it didn't involve stealing. She always vowed that if I were out in the world stealing and got caught, she wasn't coming to help me. I heard the ethical code over and over and wanted desperately to adhere to it—or, failing that, not get caught—because my mother, although she never exhibited despair, deserved no heavier burden. Sometimes she mentioned the motto of her graduating class, which was borrowed from "Life's Mirror" by the poet Madeline Bridges: "Give to the world the best that you have, and the best will come back to you." I wondered how she could believe it.

My mother helped to form a women's club that met on Tuesdays and rotated meeting venues. In other circumstances, because the spirit of helping was embedded in her personality, I could imagine my mother preoccupied with the old-style progressive club movement, casting about for ways to impact the community. When the meeting came to our home, that was our best eating day other than Sunday. The supply of spaghetti and meatballs might be unlimited. When the club sponsored dances and parties, I would often accompany her after I went to the shoe store on 102nd Street to retrieve shoes she would have dyed for the event. Her crowd liked the country side of the street when it came to soul music: Johnnie Taylor, Tyrone Davis, Betty Wright, Junior Walker & the All-Stars. I danced to a lot of "Shotgun." I think my mother had a good time at these events. She drank in moderation and had the proper restraint on her old juke-joint moves. Still attractive at thirty-nine, she drew some attention but nothing that would dramatically alter her life or ours.

When I took on two delivery routes, a morning route for the *Daily News* and an afternoon route for the *Press*, my mother cautioned me never to spend all my money. Always save. Although that was good advice, the complication was that I never got all my money because people didn't want to be bothered with the paperboy. I started collecting on Friday evenings, which started the runaround. Customers wouldn't answer the bell, or they would tell me to come back, or they said they would pay next week, even the ones already a week or two behind. Whether or not they paid, I had to turn in the same amount every week. Say on a sixty-dollar route I had to hand over forty-five dollars. If I collected forty-eight dollars, that meant I had three dollars for my labor instead of the fifteen dollars that was supposed to be my "salary." This is why I have never slighted a paperboy. Even when I have been visiting other people's homes, I have paid the paperboy. Tired of feeling exploited, I quit those routes—after I received severance pay from my cousin Terry. (Gotta tell it, T.) When Auntie dropped him off for a visit, I used to take him around the neighborhood and test him. I'd go in a convenience store with him on Northern Boulevard and, while he was looking for an item, I'd duck out and hide around the corner, watching him as he exited the store. He never panicked. He acted like he belonged, glanced up and down the Boulevard, figuring I had to be nearby. I knew we could get this paperboy money, so I handed him my books and took him, the new paperboy, to collect my routes. No more three-dollar weeks for me. The distributors probably knew what happened, but I didn't care. Terry was back home, and I never would break.

In my ninth-grade English class, we read Edwin Markham's "The Man with the Hoe." I knew nothing of the poet's reputation as the Laureate of Labor. His lines were simply unforgettable, magnetic across the gulf of time. "Bowed by the weight of centuries" . . . "And on his back the burden of the world" . . . "Never hopes." That last line wasn't me. I didn't know what I climbed toward, but I felt that I needed to be moving upward regardless of whether Markham's "whirlwinds of rebellion" would shake the world. (Or whirlwinds of revolt, as King, who read Markham, said in "I Have a Dream." We know how King liked to sample.)

At the end of a class session, a classmate asked our teacher what he thought of her college potential. Then another student asked about his prospects. This behavior was strange in my estimation because by that time I would not have set myself up like that in front of a White man. My mother told me my potential. Although my grades continued to decline, I took the Specialized High School Admissions Test in an attempt to gain admission to Stuyvesant, considered by many to be the top academic high school in the city. That whole school was SP.

But the whirlwinds could not be denied. A protester against Martin Luther King in Chicago hit him in the head with a rock. That's because, according to Mr. Boone in the barbershop, King talked about more than integration and voting. He tried to place a claim on serious resources and found the Windy City to be more hostile to him than were Alabama and Mississippi. Mr. Boone opined that such protesters in Chicago wouldn't run up that way on Muhammad Ali and the Black Muslims. Yet the establishment had ways to strike. First, it didn't respect you. I listened to the ABC radio broadcast of Ali defending his title against Cleveland Williams. So-called legendary announcer Les Keiter did the play-by-play and during the entire fight it was "Clay with a left, Clay with a right, Clay this, Clay that, still champion, Cassius Clay." Ali hadn't been Cassius Clay in almost three years. He also had not been recognized by the World Boxing Association, which stripped Ali for giving Liston a rematch. Ernie Terrell was their champ and cultural representative, continually barking "Clay." Ali shut him down soon enough but couldn't defeat government opposition. Calling him Clay all along, and rejecting religious reasons he offered as a Muslim, they hit him with harsher than usual penalties for criticizing the war in Vietnam and refusing induction into the military.

Ali was becoming an international symbol and ours, too, be it about racism, antiwar sentiment, or White authoritarianism in general. I saw pushback on Northern Boulevard on May 27, 1967. Folks were on the corner of 104th Street drinking, milling about, loudly squeezing in the last hours of a Saturday night. By the time police decided to disperse the gathering, I was already headed home. As I set out, I saw an officer try to rough up twenty-five-year-old Fred "Solitaire" Fernandez, who then swung on the cop and was arrested by several officers. That action touched off what counted as a riot in our neighborhood—bottles thrown, store windows smashed—mostly confined to the north side of the Boulevard between 104th and 105th. As the frenzy subsided, I, strictly a spectator, filed the incident away as just another night in Corona. Small compared to what would jump off that spring and summer in Tampa, Buffalo, Newark, Minneapolis, Detroit, Milwaukee, Rochester, and DC, as well as in other sections of New York City.

A few weeks later, Solitaire made the news for something more serious. Sixteen members of the Revolutionary Action Movement (RAM) were busted and charged with plotting to assassinate Roy Wilkins and Whitney Young for being "bourgeois reformists," as well as blow up a subway station and commit other acts of arson. A hefty cache of weapons, ammunition, and explosives supposedly had been seized. Solitaire was among those arrested and had his picture in the paper. Raymond Smith, also quite familiar, would appear in *Jet* magazine. This was history up close again. Some of us in school stayed in the bathroom a long time

74

reading and rereading the coverage. Solitaire and Smith weren't charged with the murder plot, only with "advocacy of criminal anarchy, conspiracy to commit arson, and violations of the weapons law."

I couldn't always identify a bourgeois reformist. I would take that puzzle to the barbershop. Reportedly, the RAM bust resulted from two years of undercover work. That part I didn't believe, which made me doubt the whole case. To me, two years of conspiring meant you weren't conspiring.

Anyway, I had a few other pressing puzzles to solve, such as getting Harry Jenkins through court. He had been one of my leaders over three years at William Cowper. He joked a lot and laughed easily at the jokes of others, but he was rugged and had a punch solid enough to crack a White boy's jaw outside the subway station on Queens Boulevard. Detectives hung around our school on two separate days before they caught him. I saw it as a shoving match that escalated—more ambiguous than what I saw on the Boulevard but not an assault. And that's what I said at the information and evidence hearing. I knew I wouldn't panic, or freeze, or get confused, or hostile, or sound too street. I could control all that.

I dressed preppy for the hearing. I wore a bright yellow button-collar shirt with a red paisley print around the inside of the collar. My tie was also a paisley print. Harry's lawyer said the tie was fine. I had been eyeing the bus to the Youth House that was parked on 89th Avenue and took up too much of the street. Cars could barely squeeze by. In front of the judge, the lawyer spoke of my clean-cut appearance while he led me through a retelling of my story. The Corporation Counsel, in conservative suit and standard cordovans, unsuccessfully tried to put words in my mouth. He tried to get me to acknowledge that I saw Harry push and then punch the White boy. What I saw was a shoving match prior to a punch. I made that clear. He next asked if I heard any racial insults used. I had not. I knew Harry's version but refrained from overtelling my story. I was only sure about what I saw. Then the Corporation Counsel gestured to the judge, and I was excused. In little more than an hour the issue was resolved. The judge ruled that there was not enough evidence to pursue the matter. I saw little of Harry in the years to come. He went his way and never got in serious trouble as far as I know. I was left to tackle Stuyvesant High.

12

My last year of junior high school was my worst in terms of grades. After trying for three years, I finally failed Spanish with a 55. Although I scored 91 on the Regents Examination in algebra, I received a 75 in math. Instead of achieving grades of 85 or above in all subjects, which was the carrot dangled before me when I entered William Cowper, I managed to earn a solitary 85, which was in English. My average in academic subjects fell to 70. Although I don't think I realized it at the time, ninth grade was considered the first year of high school in matters related to college admission. Therefore, I had completed my freshman year, two semesters, and a 70 average was no way to make it to Harvard or Yale or some other top think tank. I doubt anyone entered Stuyvesant that year with poorer grades. Nonetheless, a light clicked on for me, and I warmed to the new challenge. When I found out that colleges considered the marks for your first seven semesters, I calculated that I needed a steady run of 90s or better to get up to an 85 average. B students, especially those who overcome a bad start and demonstrate a sustained upward trajectory, can go to a decent college. My mother had asserted all summer that whatever I set my mind to I could achieve. As always, I believed her. The difference this time is that I embraced the task and admitted no distractions. The present was being set on fire. I needed to position myself for whatever the future held.

The daily three-hour round-trip commute to East 15th Street in Manhattan didn't bother me. Neither did the four or five hours of homework every night. I completed the readings for English and history, even handled the Spanish assignments. I remained focused in biology, slicing the frog and listening attentively to Miss Oliver, who, other than my few days with Mr. Frazier at JHS 16, was the only Black teacher I would ever have in public school. The precision of geometry mesmerized me. If you see the illustration clearly, you will forever have the answers. If you know the measurement of what is there, you can deduce the measurement of what is not. The sum of the squares of the other two sides equals valuable information if you intend to be college bound.

The change of scenery seemed like an arrival on a college campus. I toured the neighborhood, which went by the name Stuyvesant Square. I couldn't correctly label the Italianate or Greek Revival styles of the brick buildings and brownstone homes, but the ornate designs proved intriguing. Our school was Beaux Arts.

I would walk along 14th Street, sometimes go to the Horn & Hardart automat. Or coming over from Union Square, I might cut past Washington Irving High School, where girls, which we didn't have at all-boys Stuyvesant, milled about outside or waved from the windows. I had plenty rap by then—not really rap. Just a lame kind of approach that could sometimes work. I had learned that on any given day if you told a girl politely that she looked very nice, she mostly was going to respond by saying thank you. Then you had to read the "thank you" correctly. Could just be a keep-it-moving "thank you." Maybe not. Open the book enough and you'll comprehend. You didn't really "pull" anyway; you had to not blow the chance to be chosen.

Or I might drop down into Greenwich Village. I hadn't seen much of Lower Manhattan, mainly Orchard Street on a Sunday looking for discount clothes from Jewish merchants. We usually declared that we were going shopping on Delancey Street because that was the name of the stop on the F train. But Orchard Street was the main thoroughfare. That trip could happen with as little as five or ten dollars, which Auntie might drop on me for washing her Mustang. I might not even have to wash it if she were in a hurry—she'd pay me anyway.

A couple of students from William Cowper were at Stuyvesant. So were some PS 149 folks, including Marty Rosenberger, who was a junior because he had chosen the two-year SP option at JHS 145. We didn't get too friendly in those days. There were no invitations to visit. More important were connections with Black students such as Greg Jeffers, who ran track and occasionally rode the subway to Queens with me, and Robert Sykes from Brooklyn, with whom I discussed sports in the morning at the luncheonette adjacent to the school. Robert agonized over the New York Giants, who had not won a championship since before we started kindergarten. He was the first person I thought of when they won their first Super Bowl.

In any event, my academic plan unfolded; I had a report card befitting a former special-progress student when I averaged 87 for the first semester. I received an 80 in Spanish to follow up my 55. *Levantar.* No matter how you phrased it, I was on the rise. My mother conceded as much while reminding me that I could perform better.

Of course, despite my academic focus, the extra curriculum remained influential. Most times when I walked along 1st Avenue to the school, that is, when I happened to come in by way of the Canarsie Line, I would spot this guy on the corner, who I later found out was a senior, dressed in an army jacket and combat boots. He would pass out leaflets or pamphlets or newspapers articulating leftist viewpoints. There were always essays or articles about class oppression and the military-industrial complex. Speaking of student radicals, Mr. Boone in the barbershop said they were all socialists while their parents were footing the bills. Nonetheless, I was surprised to find a guy like that, an SDS type guy, at Stuyvesant. Seniors generally fretted most about their averages, SAT scores, and their prospects for college admission and scholarships. Yet antiwar activism increasingly surrounded me. Muhammad Ali was antiwar. Stokely Carmichael was antiwar. Martin Luther King Jr., maybe pushed by Coretta and Stokely, was antiwar. Nineteen-year-old William Gray of Corona had been killed that year in Vietnam. Rob Jones was presently in Vietnam. And I became antiwar. The chant "Hey, hey, LBJ, how many kids did you kill today?" had been around for a minute. Now active antiwar students walked on 1st Avenue. Some blended into the morning crowd outside the school entrance, a few sat alongside me in history, where the teacher and class occasionally digressed into war updates.

Secretary McNamara knew the war in Vietnam could not be won, but President Johnson and General Westmoreland erroneously thought otherwise and pressed an unsuccessful strategy of attrition. Although the defense of Khe Sanh Combat Base over the early months of 1968 and repelling the Tet Offensive during the same period were considered military triumphs, they were losses to much of the American public given the heavy U.S. casualties, as was the capture of the USS *Pueblo*. The public couldn't see the upside of more than a half million U.S. soldiers in a war half a world away, with no end in sight. For those in our mid- to late teens, that meant a draft for us on the near horizon. We were not old enough to vote for Eugene McCarthy, or even Robert Kennedy, who

78

joined the presidential sweepstakes late, but much of our support would have gone to those two.

The week after Kennedy entered the race, students at Howard University seized control of the administration building to protest racism, a Eurocentric curriculum, old-school moderation, unfair disciplinary procedures, and the war, in which a disproportionate number of African Americans served and died. The students chanted "Ungawa! Black Power!" and sought the resignation of President James Nabrit Jr. Beyond piquing my interest politically, I wondered why my Uncle James Nabrit Lewis—known as Uncle James to me, my sisters, and my cousin Terry, and as Nabrit to most others—bore the same name as Howard's president. My mother explained that President Nabrit and her father, who were about the same age, had been close friends in Georgia and that's how my uncle got his name. I accepted that story and repeated it until recently. I now think it more plausible that my uncle was named after James Nabrit Sr., who was a professor, school president, and secretary of the National Baptist Convention. In any case, had I the chance to visit or attend Howard, I doubt I would have said anything about my family story and Nabrit. Unfortunately, I blew the chance to investigate the link between President Nabrit and my grandfather. When I thought to do so, Nabrit was well over ninety years old, and I assumed he had passed. Several years afterward, I read in the obituary section of the *New York Times* that he died that week at the age of ninety-seven.

Then came the second (after the eviction) big blank in my memory. I recall nothing in terms of direct experience about the assassination of Martin Luther King Jr. The moments frozen in millions of memories are absent from mine. I don't know what I was doing, can't remember my reaction, can't recapitulate media reporting of the murder or its aftermath. I have stories told to me that provide a frame. I know Jesse Jackson kept on the bloody shirt, Aretha Franklin sang at the funeral, a tape of "Drum Major Instinct" was played, and Dr. Benjamin Mays delivered the eulogy. I'm aware that it was Maya Angelou's birthday and cities across the country burned for a few days. I know that King spoke at Convent Avenue Baptist Church and ate at Auntie's restaurant on Lenox Avenue shortly before he went to Memphis. I'm told by one of the participants that in Corona several cars packed with armed youths supposedly set out on missions along the Grand Central Parkway to shoot White people.

After everybody rendezvoused back at the starting point, they all claimed to have been unable to find suitable targets.

Maybe I'm blanking because the assassination occurred almost simultaneously with another change of residence, and I seem not to have handled descending relocations well. After a dispute with the landlord—not Mr. Bob but his wife—about plumbing nonrepairs, we ended up in a ramshackle house two blocks away. I won't use the clichés about dilapidated conditions. Suffice it to say that we were the last family to live in that structure before it was razed. It's now an empty lot where Dominicans fool around with hoopties. The landlady promised several improvements. An incomplete masonry job in front of the house is all she delivered. I intensely disliked being the courier to turn over the rent to her each month but lacked a better option. The saving grace at that address for me was that I no longer shared a room and had a semi-private spot, a seven-by-five-foot space adjoining the room where my younger sisters slept. I had to pass through their room to get to mine. I barely had enough space to stand up and turn around. The dresser blocked me from closing the door. I had a cardboard chifforobe that had been left behind, a comfortable bed, and a window. Very few people saw my room. Late at night when all else was quiet, I could hear the Number 7 train faintly rumble by on the elevated tracks a half mile away.

The aftermath of Robert Kennedy's assassination at the Ambassador Hotel in Los Angeles is more memorable. The networks combined to air twenty hours of coverage per day. I couldn't get around it or forget Kennedy's conclusion to his victory speech: "It's on to Chicago and let's win there."

I continued gaining momentum at Stuyvesant, closing with a 90.4 average for the second semester. Although I was inept at mechanical drawing, a minor subject, I received no major-subject grade below 85, obtained a 91 in Spanish, and topped out with a 94 in English. I saw 94 as a possible average moving forward. As a bonus for my mother, I scored 100 on the Regents Examination in geometry. She expressed pride in that accomplishment but did point out laughingly that it was the only 100 I had. Overall, I was doing fine.

Through the Neighborhood Youth Corps, I landed a job at Livonia Yard in East New York helping to maintain subway cars for forty-five dollars per week, thirty-eight and change after taxes. Deductions included

80

my first Social Security payments. I would offer my mother money, but she would never take it. Or if she did, she found a reason to funnel it back to me. I was spurting toward six feet and needed clothes, which I could lay away on Jamaica Avenue, where I cashed my check. The other youth workers were from Brooklyn or parts of Queens. One guy from South Ozone Park, Melvin, focused on me almost immediately, more competitive than friendly but ultimately friendly. I first had to hold him at bay. He bragged about playing in basketball tournaments in Lincoln Park. I beat him one-on-one during lunch break. He wanted to shan until I informed him that I didn't play with my hands. Then he verbally put down Corona, and I asked him if he cared to offer those opinions on Northern Boulevard. The initiation was easy enough and we were cool.

The only thing Melvin surpassed me in streetwise was snorting heroin. That shouldn't have unsettled me, but sometimes it's hard to understand what's broken inside. He never offered me any or tried to persuade me that it was hip. Yet I decided to try it back in my own neighborhood, vomiting when I first grabbed a fingernail file and used a bag, not even a whole bag. When I told Melvin about it, he expressed concern and told me not to get crazy, to sit back and think about how to proceed. He didn't feel anyone should do any more than dip and dab. You had to stay away from a habit. I snorted again that weekend and soon skin-popped, that is, took an intramuscular injection. The last destabilizing step down was the one to the main line.

We approached the secluded bleachers at 127, noticing that enough light streamed from the nearby streetlamp. Wallace rinsed out a can at the water fountain and filled it while Gary, an experienced user and the person who gave me my first hit, pulled out works that were encased in aluminum foil and tucked inside an eyeglass case. The rubber from a baby's pacifier was secured by a rubber band to the wide end of a glass eye dropper. A small spike inside a plastic case, a bottle cap with a small wad of cotton inside, and a bobby pin shaped and attached as a handle were the other major components. The bottle cap was the cooker. Gary laid down the glassine packets containing the dullish white powder. Wallace returned with the water. Gary tore off the edge of a dollar bill. We called it a g. He moistened it in his mouth before wrapping it around the open end of the dropper and jamming the wide end of the spike, still in its cover, on the dropper. He shook the dropper vigorously to make sure the spike held, then dumped the powder into the cooker before drawing about a half dropper of water from the can to squirt in. Wallace, although also a novice, knew enough to strike a match and hold the flame under the cooker. I had witnessed the procedure once or twice by then, but I remained intrigued by the chemistry and drama involved. Wallace shielded the flame with one hand like a smoker trying to light a cigarette in the wind while Gary moved the cooker in a slow circular motion to bring the contents to a sizzle. Holding the cooker with his left hand and the homemade hypodermic needle with his right, he stirred the mixture a bit while probing the cotton wad, then drew the shot by squeezing and releasing the nipple.

After I tied up above my right elbow with an elastic cord, Gary pressed his thumb hard against the vein, my most prominent one, which runs along the outside of my arm toward the crook. He exerted a downward pull to make the skin taut, then deftly pricked the skin. Blood spurted up into the dropper. Wallace released the tourniquet and Gary squeezed the injection without collapsing the nipple fully. That way he tried to avoid shooting air into the vein. He released the nipple, which caused the bloody mixture to flow back into the dropper. This was called booting, a technique to make you feel the effects of the drug faster. My head spun; my throat tasted the bitterness of the quinine used as a cut; my stomach almost flipped. Gary squirted the fluid back into the vein, squeezed the nipple all the way, and withdrew the spike. He placed his thumb near the injection spot and pressed firmly along the vein to force out any air bubbles. When finished, he walked over to the water fountain to rinse out the works. I sat dazed and began rocking back and forth, rubbing my vein.

Melvin was a mainliner by the time the summer ended. And I had fallen deeper. I told myself I could stop whenever I wanted to. Shortly after, I was on the Boulevard talking with a man, in fact the same man I hit with the stone before I hid behind my mother. While we were going over a few things, he asked how I did in school. I replied that I did okay but that it seemed sometimes like walking a tightrope. He shook his head in amusement and offered, "You got a tightrope to walk? You the luckiest kid in Queens."

13

Stress can motivate or alienate. Energize or immobilize. It's not a simple struggle. It's not, for example, about drugs all the time. Drugs are what you do in addition. You still go to school, play ball, follow the news. It's when the addition becomes too big and everything else begins to disappear that you become the person being brought down from the roof.

Back at Stuyvesant, I wished I could forgo the final two years and proceed directly to a college campus. Having a study period in my schedule, I was fortunate to be assigned to work in the college office under Myron Wechsler. I read all the information that came in about colleges, standardized tests, and financial aid. I had numerous catalogues sent to my home and arranged them neatly in the space between the foot of my bed and the wall below the window. Sometimes I lay on my bed with pen and pad calculating possible grade averages for the semester and beyond. I slipped some in the classroom but held on with at least an 85 in every major subject, averaging a shade over 88 with a 92 in trigonometry and, while reading Hawthorne's *Scarlet Letter*, another 94 in English.

Meanwhile, the noise of protests and boycotts hung in the air. The Olympics unfolded in Mexico City with former PS 90 student John Carlos helping to electrify the world when he took the bronze to Tommie Smith's gold in the men's two hundred meters and joined Smith in displaying a black-gloved Black Power salute on the victory stand while the national anthem was played. They were banned from the Olympics for life. The men's four-hundred-meter runners were craftier. When Lee Evans, Larry James, and Ron Freeman swept the medals, they donned black berets as a gesture to the Black Panthers but removed them before the anthem began. Those track athletes couldn't get flag-waving George Foreman's support, and I don't know how hard they tried. Who would step but so hard to Big George, who TKOed the Lithuanian heavyweight, Jonas Čepulis, for the gold? I would have preferred Foreman to don a black glove or beret. However, I didn't consider the nineteen-year-old Foreman an Uncle Tom, as many did.

I didn't think much at all on Election Day. Richard Nixon ascended to power on the wings of the Southern strategy: appealing to reactionary Whites in the South and Southwest, who comprised much of the so-called Silent Majority. While returns were coming in, I went out with Manuel. He had two cars along with four girls looking for adventure. I knew them all. We decided to go racing on the Whitestone Expressway. When we got to the cars, two of the girls hopped in the back seat of the car he would drive. The other two rode in the sedan with me. I think it was a Malibu. We rode out to the last exit before the bridge and circled back around to reenter the expressway. Then the race back to Corona was on. We didn't take the speed extraordinarily high but were going too fast to stop at the red light that caught us at the point where the expressway emptied onto Astoria Boulevard. Manuel, on the left, chose to run the light and beat the cross traffic. I opted to turn right down Ditmars and didn't make it, careening against a row of traffic signs and grazing several cars. Luckily no one was hurt. The girls were out in a flash. The driver's side door was jammed, which slowed my escape. As always, I thought of my mother. This was nobody using my name. This was me. I climbed into the back seat to escape and catch up with the girls. Manuel found us, and he and I walked back to peep the scene. They say we always return. A police cruiser with flashing lights had arrived.

In gym class we were expected to be in uniform every day and step lively to Mr. Davis's famous chant: "Move with alacrity. Move with alacrity." I dressed for the class occasionally and eventually failed it despite being among the better guys on gym apparatuses. Of course, failing gym served as another warning. Their number was growing larger, and the overall inevitable decline soon followed. So that spring, while Ronald Reagan was sending the National Guard into Berkeley and imposing a curfew on the town, Black students with guns held control of a building at Cornell University, the Panther 21 (or New York 21) became headlines, and my grades plummeted, I was more concerned with getting high.

As the heroin plague infested the neighborhood—a major share of the nation's quarter million heroin users lived in New York City—networks formed to get cop money. Through networks you discovered who was reliable, who was likely to snitch, who could stand the weight, even how much weight they were willing to stand. Being on the right level could be crucial. Unless you were ready to hold court on the street, you had better not get caught out there with someone who was.

One Saturday, in fact two days before Neil Armstrong and Buzz Aldrin walked on the moon, I was in possession of a shiny blue 1968 Oldsmobile Cutlass and drove for a couple of network members. This was truly hustling backward because the car was a far better asset than the proceeds of most robberies. If we had a connect to a chop shop, which wouldn't have been hard to secure, we could have obtained more money while risking less time. Anyway, I got high, hung out, and spread favors around in case I needed some on the back end. The request would be phrased "Take me to the cooker." I got home after two in the morning only to find that I was locked out. I had no key, and my mother was enforcing her new rule that if I didn't come in by a decent hour, I wouldn't be allowed in. She knew a seventeen-year-old had to have the wrong reasons for keeping the hours I wanted to keep, and she figured that I had to learn the hard way. She had the strength to stick to her word and command my sisters to go along. Barbara softened one time but not that night. On the other hand, my mother didn't have a full enough picture. It was going to take more than her new measure to rein me in.

I shrugged off my little housing problem and intended to fetch the Oldsmobile. Along the way I ran into Gary and a guy named Blue. We decided to walk over to a diner on Junction and Astoria and then proceed to 127. We ate and then bought copies of the early edition of the Sunday *Daily News*. Shortly after I settled onto a park bench to read the latest coverage about the moon mission, it began to drizzle. Instead of dashing for the car, I followed Blue when he broke into the school, going through a front window. A man walking his dog spotted us, but we paid him no mind. The police arrived a little while later.

I was sitting at a table in the cafeteria with my paper when the patrol car pulled up along 25th Avenue. Shouting an alert to Gary and Blue, who were using their newspapers as pillows, I ran for the far exit. They scrambled in the other direction toward the door closer to the window we had entered. Theirs was the poor choice, I figured, because their chosen exit was too close to the patrol car. But the police apparently caught sight of me running through the cafeteria and pulled the car up to that exit just as I burst out the door. I saw Gary and Blue getting away. Ducking back inside, I decided to dart up a stairwell and hide in the darkened fourth-floor gymnasium. That decision didn't work out either. When an officer entered cautiously, brandishing a flashlight, I was busted. Fragile and busted. He cuffed my hands behind my back and turned me over to his partner, who said I smelled like a goat. They falsely accused me of having stolen typewriters from the school. I didn't fear my mother. I had finally *failed* her. This would hurt her. No ways to dance around that fact.

At the 114th precinct, I was interviewed by a detective who seemed primarily interested in my accomplices. I insisted that I didn't know their real names and didn't know where they lived. He put on no serious pressure and said I was going up the river by myself. For arraignment, I was taken over to Atlantic Avenue in Brooklyn for weekend court and placed in a cell by myself. As one of the legal aid attorneys came down the line to do the customary interviews, the man in the next cell called to me, although I didn't realize at first that he was addressing me. "You talkin to me?" I asked apologetically. "Yeah, man. You know that punk coming here asking them questions? Don't answer him. He'll mess you up. What you got this time?" I tried to make burglary sound like murder one. Then he told the lawyer to fuck off. He had one bid in and was facing armed robbery charges in four cases. He had no prospects for probation or bail. The lawyer said that perhaps he could help. He was told, "Fuck you and leave me the fuck alone." Then he instructed me, "Don't tell him nothing, Youngblood." I told him I had to talk because I had a chance to walk. He said that made sense but warned me again that this lawyer could fuck me up.

The judge freed me early that afternoon, releasing me into the custody of my mother. That she would show up had been no foregone conclusion in my mind. The lawyer, who ironically turned out to be a Stuyvesant graduate, wondered how a fellow Peg Leg had wound up in criminal court. I sanitized the situation as much as I could, characterizing it as a little mischief. In that instance, it was. I hoped my mother perceived it that way, though I couldn't really tell. We went home mostly in silence.

Two days later I still had the car. Wallace and I went scouting for opportunities over in Elmhurst and Woodside. We took along Tango, a young neighborhood desperado who was alleged to have enough nerve. After looking at a couple of sites we thought were possible, we decided on this Chinese laundry on 31st Avenue, parking on a side block a car length or two shy of the avenue near a fire hydrant so we wouldn't get jammed in by another car. To make the getaway as smooth as possible, I left the keys in the ignition. Wallace and I exited the car, but Tango got cold feet and said he would stay behind to get the seats ready, although he was supposed to be the lookout. That was some weak-ass silly stuff, but there was no time to argue about it.

No customers were in the laundry when we entered, only the woman behind the counter who had a fit when Wallace pointed a pistol at her. She backed away slowly, shaking her head "no no no" with her palms against the sides of her face. She formed words with her mouth, but no sound issued forth. I had leaned across the counter to open the cash register when a man came in from the rear of the establishment. On seeing us his first impulse was to charge, but the image of Wallace leveling the pistol at him stifled the urge. He retreated, seemingly without fright. Sensing he was going after a weapon, I speedily grabbed a small stack of bills and scooted out the door just ahead of Wallace. We reached the bleachers at 127 in a matter of minutes. We ignored Tango until he inquired, while watching me divide the money evenly between Wallace and myself, "What about me?" His take equaled his role. Zero.

Because our haul equaled less than twenty dollars, we were scouting again later that evening. We picked up Smitty, a slight guy who was new to the pistol, as we were, but game. I actually didn't want to touch the pistol at all. We cruised back to Woodside to case targets such as bakeries, drugstores, and liquor stores. We couldn't agree to proceed.

We worked back to the east, back through Corona, then Flushing, and out to Bell Boulevard in Bayside before settling on a drugstore ripe for the picking. When the store cleared except for the proprietor, a chubby, balding White man, Wallace and I entered and approached the counter while Smitty stationed himself by the entrance. Wallace announcing a stickup didn't rattle the man at all. Without flinching, he reached under the counter. I ran for the door, held open momentarily by Wallace and Smitty. If not for the situation, I would have laughed at how they scrambled through the doorway simultaneously, seeming to make it expand like in a cartoon.

An hour or so later, we rolled along Roosevelt Avenue in Corona under the Number 7 tracks. At the corner of 111th Street, I saw a pedestrian descending the stairs from the station. Impulsively, I put the car in park and sprang. Wallace was saying no, but I paid no heed. As I pushed the man against the side of a building, thinking Wallace would be only a step behind, the police screeched to the curb. This is what Wallace had tried to warn me about. The car almost hit him as he turned and dashed back across Roosevelt. My intended victim tried to grab me, but I elbowed him and took off down Roosevelt with police in pursuit, the lights on the squad car swirling behind me.

i could not outrun the sirens. As luck would have it, I was on the longest block in the area, at least three hundred yards. The police, from the 110th precinct this time, could easily cut me off on the straightaway once they chose to pursue me instead of Wallace. Cutting into an alley, I encountered a high chain-link fence and didn't hesitate to scale it. I ripped my shirt going over but managed to jump down to the other side and scurry behind a clump of bushes just as the patrol car arrived. With his gun drawn, an officer ordered me to freeze. I wasn't planning to move anyway because I didn't figure he could see me. I was wrong again.

While I was being arraigned the next morning in Kew Gardens, the judge did a double take at my paperwork. He said it appeared as though I needed a rest and set bail at one thousand dollars. That's equivalent to over nine thousand dollars today. My mother stood alongside me. Hurt and anger twisted together in her face when she looked at me and whispered tersely, "I guess you're satisfied." She went her way, and I went the way they took me.

Auntie was my only shot at a bail bond. She assured me that she would see what she could do. In the meantime, I was taken to the Adolescent Remand Shelter on Rikers Island, cell block 5, cell 5A6. I had stomach cramps but nothing sensational like a Hollywood movie. I worried about my cases. Being caught red-handed, it wasn't like I should waste anybody's time by pleading innocent. Logically, I couldn't even be angry. I knew people doing time for offenses like those I had gotten away with.

Half the neighborhood seemed to be on Rikers, which is no surprise looking back because we were all getting high and crisscrossing the same areas. I figured that had I been a police officer, I could have caught them all. Not wanting to issue a challenge or be forced to accept one inadvertently, I avoided direct eye contact with inmates I didn't know. I hoped I could hold my own if things got that far—and uphold Corona. I heard conversations filled with lies echoing throughout the tiers. There were numerous promises of ass kickings to be delivered on the lockout.

Supposedly thirteen or fourteen months away from college, I needed to get back on track if possible. I knew dope was not the right route. That was obvious if you considered personal loss and blown opportunities. The manipulative aspect began to gnaw at my mind. An African American policeman asked me if I ever saw an ocean liner dock in Flushing Bay or a 747 land on Northern Boulevard. He overdramatized the choice of vehicles, but his point held: the neighborhood got dope because powerful people wanted the neighborhood to have it. Addicts didn't choose self-destruction. They were designed to self-destruct.

Auntie, never giving up on her nephew, sprung me in a few days. Her lecture was reasonable—and forever enshrined her verb with me: *to steer*. I don't know how her conversations with my mother went, but my mother was softer than I expected. She was upset with a neighbor who said she knew I was using but didn't tell my mother because they were friends. My mother didn't understand that kind of friendship. My father showed up the morning after I returned home. I was unaware that anybody in the family except me knew how to contact him. I was aware, on the other hand, that one person had the power to make him step up in that situation. He didn't have much to say but took me to Richmond Hill to enroll me in Samaritan House, a therapeutic community. I didn't stay, leaving shortly after he did. A couple of weeks later—I was stable in the interim—he surprised me again by taking me with him and his girlfriend on their vacation to Montreal. The plan was to keep me off the streets until the start of school. The trip proved to be a great idea. We went up on the bus and stayed in a hotel in Saint-Leonard. I remember the clean and quiet Metro, which had been in operation for about three years. I went to an Expos game. I was invited to a stag party in the room next to mine. I sipped half a glass of champagne and didn't let my father know a thing. It all felt smooth.

I returned to New York alone. My father timed my departure so I would arrive the day before the start of the school term. I had to get off the bus at the border because I had no identification, and officials had to determine what to do with me. But draft dodgers don't break into America. They break out. After a few minutes of questioning, they allowed me to reboard, and I was on my way.

14

I felt way too old to still be in high school. I felt that even if I managed my courses, was favored by the court, overcame drug involvement, and gained admission to college, I would be too worn out to attend. In any case, I sought to accumulate legal money, maybe also some wherewithal for educational expenses. I took an after-school job uptown at the arcade next to the Apollo Theater. I wore an apron with change in the front pockets to give to customers in exchange for bills. When games didn't work, mostly Skee-Ball, I jiggled a metal device called a fish in the slots, which usually worked to resolve the problem. During slow periods I became a Skee-Ball master. I had first played the game with my mother at Coney Island, rolling the balls down the middle of the lane hoping they hopped up into the 50-point bull's-eye. I learned better science at the arcade. If you hit the corner for the ricochet, you had a much better chance at the 50. It was similar to a layup in basketball; the odds were better when you used the backboard.

I could get by—with readjusted expectations, of course. No school official mentioned my legal problems, so I assumed none of them knew about the kind of essay I could write about how I spent my summer vacation. Still trying to adhere to the plan, I scored a shade under 1,200 on the SAT, not a poor performance given the circumstances. I'd get home at night while my younger sisters were trying to stay awake to watch *Divorce Court*, one of their favorite shows, and leaf through my catalogues, focusing on the University of Connecticut and the University of Notre Dame. My average now sat at 4 or 5 points lower than what I desired because I only managed an 80 average for my seventh semester. On the other hand, I averaged better than 86 for my five semesters at prestigious Stuyvesant High School, with a comparable average on Regents Examinations. Those were credentials solid enough to elicit scholarship offers from both of my preferred universities, both of which were making highly publicized efforts to recruit African American students. David Paul Robeson, a year ahead of me in school, had chosen Connecticut. I didn't know Robey (as we called him) well, or anything about his famous grandfather. However, I knew him enough to look forward to seeing him on campus. Notwithstanding, against the advice of Mrs. Hegarty, one of my English teachers, who thought the atmosphere would prove too constricting, I accepted admission to Notre Dame. My challenge was to get Notre Dame to stick with me.

During the fall semester, I failed gym again, my participation remaining unacceptable. This forced me to carry back-to-back gym classes during my eighth semester. Too often, those were the only two classes I attended. When I bothered to stick around, English was next on my schedule. I didn't really participate in that class. I might ask why books like *The Outsider* and *Manchild in the Promised Land* couldn't make the syllabus instead of *The Return of the Native*, which I declined to read. My teacher might mutter something about curriculum and the classics. I usually sat in the back row, my usual position in all classes by then. Of all things, I modeled social consciousness rhetoric into the form of the Shakespearean sonnet. That was my take on the classics. These poems were like tulips emerging from the ground after winter. I'd show them to youthful-looking Mr. Marks, who had taught me in a previous English class. He would nod his head in affirmation and encourage me to keep producing.

When I was daydreaming in class one day, a student in the next aisle patted my arm and pointed to direct my attention toward the rear door where the dean, Mr. McGinn, and my shop teacher, Mr. Valenti, peered through the thick glass. McGinn, my main antagonist in school, liked to remind me that the school in Indiana was a mere phone call away. This time he beckoned me to come out into the hall, then asked me to take a stroll with them. We walked to an empty classroom, and McGinn asked me to roll up my sleeves. I wondered how they'd put it together. Valenti's observations? But I was never high in school. Was there a court inquiry or a snitch? Whatever the case, I had no objection to the request. I rolled my sleeves up past the elbows and thrust my arms forward to indicate I had nothing to hide. Let them show me what they knew. McGinn examined my left arm, the one hardly pricked, and the right arm, where there was scar tissue along the thickest vein from repeated puncturing and discernible needle marks.

"So you're using dope," stated McGinn.

"Used to."

They stepped to the side and whispered between themselves before ushering me across the street to be examined in the emergency room at

Beth Israel Hospital. I think they were primarily interested in whether I was presently under the influence, which I was not. The physician checked my eyes and reflexes. He asked a few questions and engaged me in conversation to gauge my degree of alertness. He left me in the waiting room in emergency for an hour or so before informing me that I was free to leave. Actually, I didn't need permission, didn't even have to cooperate or even go there in the first place. I was just tired. That night I assured my mother that I hadn't committed any new transgressions. She had hope because she had seen my acceptance letters and knew I was working. Plus, the hours I was keeping were sensible.

The next day the guidance counselor, Mrs. Brody, summoned me for a lengthy talk. She was a nice, engaging person who treated me like I was grown. We had a realistic exchange about things. She suggested, though not in an overbearing way, that I participate as an outpatient at Greenwich House, a rehabilitation center over on 14th Street off 6th Avenue. I went for the intake interview and talked with a counselor but chose not to enroll.

I was around school even less frequently after that, heading toward fifty-six official absences for the eighth semester alone. I put in more hours on my job and had no interest in everyday attendance again until the U.S. invaded Cambodia and the National Guard gunned down four antiwar students at Kent State University. Protests were held in Union Square and at Stuyvesant, where students staged a walkout. An assembly was called—I remember Mr. Marks being there—and students blew off steam before settling back into business as usual. They settled too soon in my view. Eleven days after the Kent State massacre, police fired on a crowd of protesters at Jackson State College in Mississippi, killing law student Phillip Gibbs and high-schooler James Green, a bystander. I thought it time for at least one more demonstration at school, but students, edging closer to finals or graduation, didn't disrupt classes again, although I recall some agitated brothers and some broken windows.

After the fervor faded, the most incredible fact of my senior year stared me in the face. It was still possible to graduate. After I'd made several appearances in court, my case was coming to a head. Two matters needed resolution. One, I had to take a drug test at the facility on Edgecombe Avenue. An old head from the Boulevard told me that to make sure I tested negative I should drink a bottle of vinegar. I figured vinegar in small doses wasn't harmful. After all, people used it on salads and to dye Easter eggs. Drinking a whole bottle, though, was out of the question. I didn't get halfway. Two, a decision had to be made about my status as a youthful offender. I had two cases when you usually got only one bite at the apple.

I cleared court on June 3. With my father in attendance, I was indeed given youthful offender treatment. In exchange for pleading guilty, my record would remain sealed if I encountered no further legal trouble. After sentencing, the judge reminded me of the opportunities before me and instructed me emphatically to go to school, live up to my potential, and stay out of her courtroom. My lawyer took us to his office across Queens Boulevard to transact business with my father. While we were there, he asked to speak to me in private. He told me it was okay to smoke a joint or two; it was the best thing for loosening up. But he cautioned against the hard stuff, calling it bad news.

I could make no decent grades for the eighth semester. I was in worse shape than when I left William Cowper three years earlier. Furthermore, because of my poor attendance record, I was technically ineligible to take the required Regents Examinations in physics, history, and English. However, Mrs. Brody cleared the path. She asked me if I could guarantee that I would pass the exams. When I assured her that was the case, she consulted with the appropriate people to make it possible for me to take the three exams. Only physics required much study because the course was specific to that school year. You couldn't bank on getting by based on knowledge accumulated over a long period of time. At any rate, I delivered on my guarantee with scores of 82 on the physics exam, 79 on the history, and 83 on the English.

All was in order except in English. Despite passing the Regents, my teacher gave me a failing grade of 40 because of all the time and work I had missed. Mrs. Brody resolved that problem as well. On the last day of school, June 23, after every other student had left the premises, it was decided in a special meeting that the Regents grade, what the state cared about, was the trump card. The 40 remained, but I was given credit for the course and allowed to graduate. I did so the next day at Carnegie Hall—my mother on the lower level, my father in the balcony.

Attending college in the fall was improbable. I told myself not to head to Notre Dame addicted, but the way I got high that summer, you could only conclude that I intended to kick on the bus ride to South Bend. But it didn't even matter after the president of the university, Father Theodore Hesburgh, sent me a letter canceling my admission. He said I was unprepared for college at that time. He surely knew what he was talking about. My attendance record and a 64 average indicated more than just a case of senioritis. I wondered if my old friend the dean had called the university.

My mother received the news stoically, almost as though she had expected it. She was probably thankful not to hear worse. I think my father had been more adventurous in his dreaming, so he appeared to be more dismayed, at least outwardly. We called Connecticut to see if their offer could be reactivated. That was impossible because the scholarship had been awarded to someone else.

There would be no college for me in August. The White folks with whom I'd put in all that time could finally leave me behind, a bad enough defeat. But I felt I had let the brothers down. Even as we ran together, several of them depended on me to win. This was the perspective of eighteen-year-old Wallace, for example, recent recipient of a three-year sentence for robbery. He kept writing to tell me to tighten up the school thing and do better.

I found encouragement in the streets also. Alan Jennings, a tough survivor in his own right, was on his way to Queensborough Community College. I had known Alan since I first came on the block in 1963. His house was my first stop when I started my brief stint at JHS 16. We walked together to school and had been assigned to the same class. Over the years, Alan, one of the most positive people you could ever hope to meet—a definite mind-over-matter guy—always had a pep talk. He urged me to apply for January admission. A few other friends, such as Gene Gatewood, who had been on the block before his family moved to Jamaica, also would be on hand. Alan's plan for me was that I put in a few good semesters at Queensborough and then keep following my potential. Naturally, I would have to cease with the drugs. But when I tried to quit, I caught a cramp and went back into the cooker. A newspaper story, no real surprise, yanked me out for good.

On August 8 the papers reported that seventeen-year-old Jonathan Jackson walked into the Marin County Hall of Justice in California with guns attempting to set in motion a chain of events that would lead to the release of the three Soledad Brothers—John Clutchette, Fleeta Drumgo, and Jonathan's brother, celebrated prison writer George Jackson. Jonathan disrupted the trial of James McClain and, with the assistance of McClain and witnesses William Christmas and Ruchell Magee, took hostage Judge Harold Haley, prosecutor Gary Thomas, and three jurors. Jonathan was killed in the subsequent shootout along with Haley, McClain, and Christmas.

Most people on the street were buzzed about the derring-do and the fireworks. Most significant to me was Jonathan's age. A kid younger than I put his life on the line because he believed in revolutionary dreams and really thought he could pull off the maneuver at the courthouse. I understood dreams, idealism, living in the future. But you have to know when the future has arrived. Or as Abiodun Oyewole of the Last Poets would say, "Time is running out of time."

Almost as soon as I finished reading the story, I knew that I was done with the drug life. It wasn't logical, but revelations aren't. The truth of my change was as clear to me as the bright caps of angry ocean waves hurtling toward shore—a rhythmically sparking clarity to which one who is amid the turbulence of the sea would be blind. That same afternoon I went to my father's apartment. After watching a baseball game on television, I announced that I would hang around and spend the night. Pops was at the post office on 34th Street by then working the night shift. I had helped him with math to prepare him for the exam. He landed the job, his best after bouncing around for years, just in time to make twenty years by the age of sixty-five. Now I needed from him the solitude to also get on track.

I took on the stomach cramps, the runny nose, the diarrhea, and the chills alternating with outbursts of sweat. The first night was sleepless, but as I rolled across the sheets I welcomed the struggle. I imagined fluorescent peaks of those waves crashing just before me. I conjured up images I hadn't gathered myself to decipher. I saw the yo-yo heads bobbing up and down in nods of escapism. They decorated Northern Boulevard, Lenox Avenue, 8th Avenue, and Avenue D. I saw gorgeous women transformed into apparitions of slurred speech and desperate thighs. I saw everyone scratching, lazily slapping their own faces. I saw yellow-eyed hepatitis sufferers and spike marks in necks and alongside vaginas. I saw the drops of blood on my diploma because I got careless while showing it off to win a bet about having graduated. I recalled shoving ice down Gary's underwear after he overdosed. I shot salt water into his arm and walked him back to consciousness. He had to figure it out from there.

I was on my way to college.

15

I prowled for radical and energetic ideas. Straight gobble-up mode. After repeatedly walking past it during the first year after it was opened, I began to post up at the Langston Hughes Community Library & Community Cultural Center on Northern Boulevard. I was in the real world. Much of that which streamed by on the street beyond the large front window represented a parallel universe, a bizarro land, recognizable but filled with reversals and other moves that were slightly off.

I consumed almost all the Black poetry the library had on hand, works such as *Black Fire*, edited by Amiri Baraka and Larry Neal; *The New Black Poetry*, edited by Clarence Major; *We Speak as Liberators*, edited by Orde Coombs; and *Soulscript*, edited by June Jordan. I also kept track of the slim volumes coming from Broadside Press and Third World Press, which I jumped on as if they were the latest soul records. That's how I first read the poetry of Marvin X, Doughtry Long, Carolyn Rodgers, Johari Amini, Nikki Giovanni, Jayne Cortez, Don L. Lee (later known as Haki Madhubuti), and others associated with the Black Arts Movement. Lee veered close to my sense of the streets as he saw in his neighborhoods what I saw in mine. Moreover, humor laced his poetry, a quality that had to be present in some degree for the work to seem authentic to me. Our lives are never only grim. In poems such as "But He Was Cool," "A Poem to Complement Other Poems," and "Black Sketches," I perceived the mix of serious social criticism and the comedic. Also evident was the debt to Langston Hughes's "I, Too, Sing America" displayed in "They Are Not Ready." In addition to poems, Lee wrote insightful introductions. In *Think Black!* he wrote, "The Black writer learns from his people and because of his insight and 'know how' he is able to give back his knowledge to the people in a manner in which they can identify, learn and gain some type of mental satisfaction, e.g., rage or happiness." This thinking squared with that incorporated by Malcolm X into "Statement of Basic Aims and Objectives of the Organization of Afro-American

Unity." He established the group after his separation from the Nation of Islam. Malcolm spoke of a cultural revolution in which artists draw inspiration from their community and the community supports those artists. Lee also spoke pointedly in *We Walk the Way of the New World* about an identity that was on my mind: Black college student. He classified students as either unserious or serious, the former given to frivolity and individualism, the latter being committed to themselves *and* their people. The latter role sounded right. In contrast, I found nothing wrong with slight indulgence in the "ripple, reefer, and rappin'" against which Lee railed.

On separate occasions, Nikki and Jayne came to the library to read. Nikki's reading captivated the audience—everyone thirsted for the exciting "Ego Tripping," with its Langston-like (he's everywhere) "The Negro Speaks of Rivers" echoes. She offered commentary about a writing career. From her I learned about a kill fee, that is, money that a magazine paid if it contracted for an article but decided in the end not to publish it. For "killing" the piece, the magazine paid half of the original amount to the writer. I have never had to use that information. It just felt exciting to be put on game. Jayne placed me under a lifelong spell. Radiant and majestic, she read mostly from *Pissstained Stairs and the Monkey Man's Wares.* Selections included "Lead," "Dinah's Back in Town," and "How Long Has Trane Been Gone?" I thereafter caught every Jayne Cortez performance I could.

After exhausting the recent poetry holdings in the library, I would embark on a relentless search for titles the library didn't have. I went uptown to Michaux's on 125th Street and the Liberation Bookstore on Lenox Avenue. I ran down material coming out of the east in Bedford-Stuyvesant. In addition, I scooped up albums by the Last Poets (*The Last Poets*), the Original Last Poets (*Right On!*), Gylan Kain (*The Blue Guerrilla*), Wanda Robinson (*Black Ivory*), and Gil Scott-Heron (*A New Black Poet*). Scott-Heron, I learned, drew inspiration from seeing the Last Poets perform at Lincoln University while he attended that institution.

Naturally, I couldn't ignore earlier generations, not in the Langston Hughes Library with *The Langston Hughes Reader* staring me in the face. I read all of his masterpiece *Montage of a Dream Deferred* and dabbled in Simple stories such as "There Ought to Be a Law" and "Two Sides Not Enough."

Gwendolyn Brooks offered a blend of the old and contemporary. I knew she was important and a recognized formal master but, aside from "Of De Witt Williams on His Way to Lincoln Cemetery," "We Real Cool," and "The Ballad of Rudolph Reed," I didn't have as much patience with *Selected Poems* as I would later. Brooks published *Riot* as part of the Broadside juggernaut. I was more in tune with that volume back then.

Robert Hayden does not play fair in "Runagate Runagate": "Runs falls rises stumbles on from darkness into darkness." He has "stum" and "from" to echo the sound of "runs." He has the letter *r* stretched across the line. The sound of *s* occupies six spots. The *l* in *stumbles* picks up the *l*s in *falls*. He repeats *darkness* for rhythm. And he does all this in nine words. It was the best opening line of poetry I had ever read. The closing line ain't bad either: *Mean mean mean to be free.* In fact, I have been so intrigued by the entire poem for years that I created an erasure poem, using only Hayden's words: *blackness ahead / keep on going / freedom-bound / from Can't to Can / keep on going now or die / Harriet Tubman / calling in the ghosted air / Midnight Special / first stop Mercy / the last Hallelujah.*

Most of the recent poetry I read reflected cultural nationalism. That held positive emotional value for me, but my political frame of reference was Panther-like, employing a critique that considered class as well as ethnicity. Just as I didn't think you needed to destroy the entire "white thing," which Neal argued, I didn't think you needed to be dichotomous or rule out all coalitions. For example, reparations were called for by both cultural nationalists and the Marxist-Leninist Panthers. How were they to be secured? I saw mostly a common agenda when I reviewed the Panthers' Ten-Point Program. (I weekly bought the paper for twenty-five cents.) In the activist community, a proposal for a guaranteed income wasn't controversial. Even Martin Luther King Jr. wanted that. Decent housing, meaningful education, community control, free health care, the end of police brutality, and opposition to imperial wars constituted a solid agenda for both camps. As for the divide, some argued that a cultural revolution was paramount because such activity developed the mindset to enact a political revolution, while their counterparts asserted that a political revolution had to occur first because it was the only way to ensure that a cultural revolution could be sustained. As for the Panthers' idea that all Black and poor oppressed people should be released from jails and prisons, I couldn't wrap my head around that as a good idea or relate unequivocally to the slogan "Off the Pig."

So I'm sifting through poetry and politics when Helen Marshall strikes up a conversation. Always about the community, this is the same woman who was involved in protesting the attack on Black students in Astoria, and who would also become the first Black person elected borough president of Queens. She was on the staff of the library and curious about my frequent visits. I told her I worked the night shift, eleven to seven, on the Port Authority maintenance crew at LaGuardia Airport but was thinking about going to Queensborough. She said there was no need to think. The City University of New York, of which Queensborough was a unit, was tuition free, and she would provide the application. She was puzzled when I revealed where I had attended high school but didn't press me about it. She just told me to keep moving forward.

This was the same thing Ted Kennedy told me. I was slinging a mop in the Eastern Airlines corridor, what we called Finger 4, when Kennedy came along looking for the boarding gate so he could catch the late-night flight to Washington, DC. He had been to a fancy fundraiser in town and was red in the face and unsteady on his feet. He wasn't all the way tore down, but it's a good thing he wasn't driving to Chappaquiddick. As I helped him to the gate, making sure he didn't slip on my floor, he asked me what I was up to besides mopping. I told him I was about to go back to school. He considered that a good idea.

Although I was indeed ready to move on to become a full-time daytime student with a work-study job to get by, my airport days were fun. While each airline had a janitorial crew, the Port Authority covered the common areas. The fingers, meeting the senator notwithstanding, were not the place to be because you worked them in pairs, sometimes trios if the floor had to be stripped. None of the tasks took more than four hours if you hustled. However, on the fingers, because you worked as a team, you couldn't finish faster than your partners, and the older guys did everything by the book. You wouldn't finish until after six. With a solo detail, you could be done by three o'clock and retreat to one of your hiding spots, like the chapel. There was an unstated agreement that if your work was on point and you stayed out of sight, things were cool. You could nap or doodle poetry in a memo pad or smoke some weed. Therefore, when I drew the bathrooms, rugs, or chrome, I maxed them so that the supervisor kept assigning me to the same detail until my day off and let me reclaim it when I returned. No one was more reliable. I especially had the escalators on lock. As I wrote years afterward when I ran into an old friend at the airport: *washington still had the escalators spotless / in the main terminal of laguardia airport / claimed to be the best ever / as we laughed and embraced / he was only second best / i knew.*

In January 1971, when I took the required placement exams, I got my first look at Queensborough, nestled among the hills and valleys of the former Oakland Country Club in relatively privileged Bayside, Queens. I would learn in an English class that from campus you could peep across the city line into Jay Gatsby territory in even more privileged Nassau County. At the exams I ran into Charles Gray, the younger brother of Vietnam casualty William Gray. He gave me a lift back to Corona.

I had three more steps. One, register for class. Two, with my last paycheck buy a family ring, containing five birthstones, to present to my mother. Three, handle Manuel. He had a car stashed in Flushing and asked me to bring it to Corona. Such actions were no longer supposed to be a part of my world. That I would ride in a stolen car with Manuel and then drive one for him defied all logic—except the logic of a street bond. I was driving along Kissena Boulevard near Queens College when I heard the siren behind me. It only took a trembling instant to realize it was a fire engine trailing me, not the police. My final warning. Twenty years before Tre's wise "let me out" moment in *Boyz n the Hood*, I eased over to let the truck pass and began to look for a parking space. I told a bewildered Manuel, "Can't fuck with it. See you when I see you." And I turned down the offer of a lift. I had spoken—and later spoke for Manuel in a poem. *i didn't dig it at the moment / because even i couldn't drive two cars / at the same time / but i do understand why he quit halfway.* When my car was stolen and police caught the teenager who did it, I didn't press charges. I told an officer to tell the kid to take advantage of the break. I can't square up everything, but I try.

When I walked down a hallway in the Humanities Building the first day of the semester, I heard all this commotion. It was cheerleading practice, a dress rehearsal, though not the typical bobby-socks, pom-pom style. These were sisters decked out in bright-colored buba blouses and dresses along with matching geles. Beautiful young women preparing to cheer on the Simbas, the Queensborough entry in the Brothers Basketball

League. The organization, an alternative to traditional varsity programs, had a political platform that revolved around championing education and celebrating Black culture. With respect to African influences, the Simba cheerleaders were the best representatives in the league.

I enrolled in two courses dealing with communication: English Composition I and Voice and Diction. The writing course presented no problems. I had much to say and little difficulty being fluent. I didn't feel oppressed by the institution's language or daunted by the task of writing myself into academic conversations. Whatever the assignment was, I was inclined to follow Langston Hughes's "Theme for English B" and bend the task to my purposes. The overriding concern for me was the relevance of our coursework to Black liberation. Writing had to mean something to me, as it always had, if I were going to compose with meaning in academe. When I became an English tutor at QCC and tried to help students correct their "errors," I habitually delivered pep talks. They thought writing came easy to me or was a gift. I knew it had more to do with reading and work and practice and a sense of high stakes.

Voice and Diction became the obstacle after I failed the speech test. At the placement taping, I softened the initial consonant cluster for words like *these*, *there*, *their*, and *those* and dragged out the vowel sound in *rice* and *ice*. The examiner decided that I needed a remedial course to address my southern accent. This was the fate of nearly all the other African American first-year students at QCC, mostly all of whom were northerners. To us, a southern accent meant "sounding country," which we didn't. Nonetheless, the professor spun me around and got me to play the game for a while. I stood in front of the mirror over-articulating and trying to inculcate a habit of saying *these* instead of *dese*. Only immersion could make much difference on that front—if I were, in fact, invested in the immersion. I doubted *rice* and *ice* would ever change. At any rate, I soon quit doing the exercises, although I finished the course, unlike several of my African American classmates. At the post-semester taping, I glared at the professor and spoke pretty much as I had before. I passed the course.

Back then I hadn't read Beryl Bailey, Lorenzo Turner, or William Stewart. J. L. Dillard's *Black English* was yet on the horizon, and Geneva Smitherman's *Black Language and Culture: Sounds of Soul* was a couple of years further off. I didn't know I spoke a systemic, rule-governed variety of English called Ebonics. About fifteen years after my time at QCC, I spoke at a language symposium held there about my time in remedial speech. My old professor happened to be in attendance and told the audience it was impossible that I had been in such a class at QCC. Of course, his pronouncement ran against the evidence the registrar could have provided. I am always reminded that my C+ in Voice and Diction was awarded simultaneously with my A– in English Composition I. Because of this I remain suspicious when folks try to blame writing problems on so-called dialect. The analysis should focus, to the contrary, on questions of purpose, prior experiences, motivation, and perceptions of institutional texts and subtexts.

Back at the library, we started a poetry workshop, which included Ahmasi, Randy Latimer, Eric Rawlins, Lorraine Taylor (our best poet), me, and a few others. We organized poetry shows featuring ourselves as well as other poets from the community. Sometimes people dashed in from the street, grabbed the microphone, and improvised poems, many wine-induced. Hip-hoppers call it free-styling. And it was cathartic, line after line about Black kings and queens and about how we'd live large when the crackers and honkies were placed in tip-top check.

I took my improvising beyond the library. Hanging out at the Village Vanguard with Maurice Ford, one of my main QCC running buddies, I scribbled a poem on a napkin and gave it to McCoy Tyner after a set. He accepted it graciously and politely tucked it away. I don't know the fate of that text. However, those few lines were the seed of several poems about Tyner over the years. *stretching lungs of piano so they scream / the long wail of open sore truth.*

The library hosted a small community newspaper, the *Corona–East Elmhurst Transition Press*, which was sponsored by the *New York Times* Community Journalism Workshop and the New York City Parks, Recreation, and Cultural Affairs Administration. The young staff, including Clarice Hunter, Vincent James, Venetta Jarvis, Raymond Pennerman, Calvin Pitter, and Eric Rawlins, had been producing insightful content since the publication's founding two years prior. Part of the *Times* support involved sending newspapermen to show us the journalistic ropes. We were coached by the likes Al Harvin, who reported on the Watts rebellion for the Associated Press and now covered sports for the *Times*, and John Darnton, who would win a Pulitzer Prize for international reporting. Each person who attended the Saturday morning sessions received five dollars, not an insignificant contribution to Saturday night festivities. Photographers were given free rolls of film.

Our neighborhood comprised a microcosm of Black urban America. For example, in just a five-block stretch of Northern Boulevard, say from 100th Street to 105th Street, there were several liquor stores where winos lined up in the morning, rampant drug activity around the clock, storefront Christian churches, the liberal Walter White social service center, the Nation of Islam Temple 7B, the headquarters of a branch of the Black Panther Party, and the library. In addition, you could observe in the neighborhood the tensions between homeowners and the permanent underclass, rifts among the working class, petit bourgeois, and "illegitimate capitalists." You could trace movements of students going to and from colleges, Ivy League students as well as community college students.

In the spring of 1971, the Black Panthers were falling apart from infighting, with agent provocateurs undoubtedly serving as catalysts. Through most of 1970, everything had been "Free Huey!" Moreover, he was generally celebrated by the membership when he visited New York. However, a rift in organizational vision, especially between Newton and Eldridge Cleaver, in exile in Algiers, occurred and was exacerbated by Newton expelling several dissenters, including the Panther 21 (reduced to the Panther 13), who had been on trial for nearly two years after being indicted—156 charges altogether—for allegedly conspiring to commit assassinations and bombings. All defendants were acquitted of those charges later in the spring. Meanwhile, the infamous Newton-Cleaver phone call took place, during which Newton called Cleaver a punk and indicated that he would deal with their disagreements with guns. Shortly after, Cleaver loyalist Robert Webb was killed in Harlem on March 8, and Newton devotee Sam Napier was slain in Corona on April 17 at the branch office between 101st and 102nd. The building was set ablaze. I was two blocks away on the Boulevard that Saturday when firefighters were on the scene. I thought it was only a fire, not a murder scene. At the time, I was unaware of the specific events leading to the recent violence among Panthers. I told a numbers runner on my block that White folks got Webb and Napier. He replied that I shouldn't turn White folks into God. They do their share but can't do it all. Only much later did I learn of a March 14 communiqué. Released six days after the Webb murder from the Bronx office over the signature of Diahnne Jenkins, billed as the communications secretary of the Black Panther Party's New York State chapter, the statement denounced Newton, David Hilliard, and June Hilliard as counter-revolutionaries and charged that Newton and David Hilliard "planned, ordered, and executed" the murder of Webb and had thus incurred a debt that "can only be paid in blood." The New York chapter recognized the Central Committee to consist of Chairman Bobby Seale (imprisoned in Connecticut at the time), Minister of Information Eldridge Cleaver, Field Marshal Don Cox, and Communications Secretary Kathleen Cleaver. This dissident perspective expressed by Jenkins would soon have deep resonance to me. However, my final take is that we'll probably never get a full accounting of what transpired. Indeed, dangerous factions existed. It's also true that one should not underestimate the damage done by COINTELPRO, the FBI's counterintelligence program created to neutralize groups the government perceived to be subversive. My witness regarding the Black Panthers is that I saw them working on programs for the community around food, health, and safety issues.

That spring I also followed closely the actions of a resurgent Muhammad Ali, who had regained boxing privileges. Incidentally, on the same day Webb was killed, Ali lost to Joe Frazier in the Fight of the Century. Of course, it didn't deserve that billing if you considered the other things going on. Not only was the result disappointing from a sports perspective (for a long time, I erroneously contended that Ali really won the bout), harder to swallow was that a supporter of Frank Rizzo, a police chief synonymous with anti-Black police brutality in Philadelphia, had taken down the Greatest.

I felt better when I saw Ali at Queens College. Jacques DeGraff, now the Reverend Jacques Andre DeGraff, suggested that we attend the event. Jacques, a couple of years older than I, seemed to be in the middle of everything at Queensborough and have connections everywhere. He said we could go backstage, and I didn't doubt him because Jacques had that presence. We ended up standing behind the curtain in Colden Auditorium, about twenty feet from Ali while he spoke. We mostly saw his back and broad shoulders that strained against his sports coat (maroon, I think). I thought no one that big should be that fast. As part of his presentation, Ali performed an original poem in which a Black revolutionary makes his last stand against the police. "Better far from all I see / To die fighting to be free / What more fitting end could be?" His opening was reminiscent of Claude McKay's "If We Must Die." Ali continued a few stanzas later, "Better far that I should go / Standing here against the foe / Is there sweeter death to know?" He closed the poem, "Better now than later on / Now that fear of death is gone / Never mind another dawn." After the closing line, Ali burst into a simulation of a combatant wielding a machine gun, sound effects and all. He seemed to have absorbed some of the impulses of mentor poets, including Hughes and Baraka, and to have contributed to setting the militant edge of Black Arts poetry. Not many in the crowd would have chosen the path indicated in the poem, but they ate up the presentation. I did not get to speak with Ali. If Jacques managed to, I wouldn't be surprised.

Jacques took me to meet another poet, Sonia Sanchez, whose *Homecoming* and *We a BadddDDD People* I had read. Her persona expressed "who's gonna make all / that beautiful blk rhetoric / mean something." This was a political plea, a call to move beyond slogans and work concretely toward Black empowerment within an anti-capitalist context. The persona wanted action. To be sure, both Sanchez and I knew that injecting "beautiful blk rhetoric" into literary and public spaces constituted a significant accomplishment. She conducted a workshop on Sundays, or maybe it was just that Sunday, at the National Black Theatre on 125th Street in Harlem. A commanding presence despite her slight stature, she held us spellbound with her radiance, magnetism, and flair. As part of the proceedings, she read a poem about a five-cent sour pickle, the kind we bought from a lot of candy stores. She took a mundane object and created a poem around it, a lesson about discipline, focus, and possibilities of the everyday, voiced, of course, in her inimitable style.

There was no immediate payoff to attending the poetry workshop. I couldn't compose well enough to snag the girl I chased around campus all semester. *we all go through these crazy perfections.*

16

My short article about the justice system, accompanied by a photo of Angela Davis, who was charged with involvement in the Jonathan Jackson episode, ran in the July 12, 1971, issue of the *Transition Press*. Regarding the acquittal of the Panther 13 and the dismissal of the cases against Bobby Seale and Ericka Huggins as mere "malfunctions" of a generally oppressive judicial machine, I noted Attorney General John Mitchell's June 9 remarks before the National District Attorney Association that the Nixon administration planned to propose legislation to end the "preoccupation with fairness for the accused." I closed by reminding readers that *they*, the justice system, still had Angela. My article failed to satisfy the purposeful twenty-three-year-old woman who came by the library inquiring about the author. I happened to be on hand and was told politely but firmly about my misstep, although I don't recall exactly how I failed in her estimation. Her general criticism was that, although it was positive that I paid attention to the Panther trial and Davis, she felt I could have said more. Seeing that I wasn't defensive, she spread the newspaper on the table before us and pointed to phrases that should have been amplified or worded more strongly. That was Diahnne Jenkins of the communiqué. It turned out she worked in the library's tutoring program that summer, as did I. When she had time, she advised me about raising my philosophical and political consciousness. According to her, that was the road to becoming a better journalist or any other kind of writer. She led me to reading Frantz Fanon, Herbert Marcuse, a former teacher of Davis, and Maurice Cornforth. I didn't come close to grasping all the nuances. I settled for underlining basic concepts for myself.

Concerning the psychology of oppression, I perused Frantz Fanon's *Black Skin, White Masks*, in which he provided elaborate descriptions of racism, colonialism, and the "massive psychoexistential complex" he hoped to obliterate, which meant, in part, analyzing his own coping with racial trauma. Although attuned to Négritude poets such as Léopold

Senghor, David Diop, and above all his teacher Aimé Césaire (I had to read them), he ultimately argued for a personal freedom that extended beyond the boundaries of racial chauvinism. As he indicated, he could appreciate that some Negro philosopher corresponded with Plato but didn't see how that fact changed the lives of child laborers in the cane fields of Martinique or Guadeloupe. But I countered that being aware of the Negro philosopher could influence what child laborers in cane fields thought possible to achieve.

I followed with Fanon's *The Wretched of the Earth*, a perennial item on the Black Radical Bestseller List. The book owed its popularity partly to the author's analysis and justification of violence in dismantling colonization. Any act of violence against a colonial representative or asset was deemed heroic. It was a zero-sum game for Fanon. Decolonization, the toppling of ruling outsiders, had to be achieved by force, by "red-hot cannonballs and bloody knives." I found Fanon's logic compelling but did not see his work as a prescription for exploited Black people in America's urban ghettoes. The ghettoes were not Algeria, no matter how many times they were defined *as* colonies or defined to be *like* colonies. After all, metaphors and similes break down under serious scrutiny because the first object isn't, in fact, the second object. On the other hand, I saw value in righteous anger transformed into armed resistance. Only Fanon's "colonized intellectual" could miss that point. Although "our" struggle needed to come into sharper focus for me, I did appreciate Fanon's remarks about poets—their writing should be in service of the people.

In *An Essay on Liberation*, Marcuse spoke of the Great Refusal, the decision by people to oppose corporate capitalism, the "cruel affluence" of the Establishment. He explained the prime imperative of capitalists—creating and reaping surplus value—and pointed to forms their initiatives assumed domestically and abroad. He also wrote of a rupture in the linguistic universe of the Establishment marked by occurrences such as the redefining, negating language of Black militants. He argued that the Black Panthers (while not naming them directly) referred to state officials as "pigs" to remove them from the role of public servant in the minds of the Panthers' audience. He considered the inversion of "soul," which he asserted had been a lily-white concept dating back to antiquity. "Soul," according to Marcuse, had migrated to Negro culture and was "black, violent, orgiastic," and to be found "in the blues, in jazz, in rock 'n' roll, in 'soul food.'" The only thing I thought Marcuse missed is that we were no longer "Negroes." On poetry, Marcuse provided a counterpoint to Fanon. Although he and Fanon agreed on the import of Black music, Marcuse, unlike Fanon, did not view poetry as simply instrumental or subservient to materialism or politics. In his view, poetic truth and imagination need not be validated by the material. Being for artistic freedom, I liked the provision by Marcuse even while on many days I thought of poetry as Fanon did.

With Cornforth's *Materialism and the Dialectical Method*, I arrived at a version of the cultural revolution vis-à-vis political revolution question or, in another form, does consciousness shape material conditions or do material conditions shape consciousness? It's a theoretical problem I certainly never solved. I grasped the assertion that everything had a materialist base, even the unknown. But how could you prove anything about the unknown while it remained unknown? Materialism focuses on human agency. I felt that was positive. Also useful was the notion of dialectics, a way of understanding that development was driven by contradictions and negations in the social order. This related to the question of whether race or class constituted the fundamental contradiction for Black people. I never signed on to either/or. The ruling class wasn't colorless—or ungendered, for that matter. And the ruling class could be multicolored and multigendered. In any event, I didn't see dialectical materialism leading to a dictatorship of the proletariat. This sounded like a God-concept and required as much faith.

Because of my exuberance, I became everybody's favorite student. I ducked people so I could catch up with my reading before they added titles to my list. Furthering an international perspective, I read Aimé Césaire's *Discourse on Colonialism* and his classic poem *Return to My Native Land*. Oh, Césaire: "My mouth shall be the mouth of misfortunes which / have no mouth, my voice the freedoms of those freedoms / which break down in the prison-cell of despair." I holed up with Nkrumah's *Neo-Colonialism: The Last Stage of Imperialism* and *Consciencism*, his philosophical treatise on how African society, grappling with the contradictions of the modern African conscience, could incorporate Western, Islamic, and Euro-Christian elements into a socialist program for a union of independent African states.

At the library with us that summer was poet, playwright, and drama consultant Farrell J. Foreman, a Villanova University student. Farrell had published a poetry chapbook and was building a stage and installing lighting as part of the renovation of the second floor. In the sanctuary that the library was, Diahnne read his book and poetry by Neal, Lee, and several others. Those moments had to be less intense for her. After denouncing Huey Newton publicly (I hadn't yet seen the March 14 communiqué), Diahnne possessed a healthy paranoia. One day on the Boulevard, she held a copy of *Right On!*, the newspaper of the New York faction. She wrote for the publication as she had previously for the *Black Panther*. A man she knew approached aggressively and asked her, "Shouldn't you be reading the other paper?" He really meant you *should be* reading the other paper. After he left, Diahnne was quiet and shaken for a while—and guarded in general.

We kept the *Transition Press* going, the biggest local story that summer being the passing of Louis Armstrong, the greatest jazz musician who ever lived. After his body lay in state for two days at the Seventh Regiment Armory in Manhattan, the funeral took place in the modest Corona Congregational Church at 103rd Street and 34th Avenue, a block from the library. The service was mostly for a few hundred celebrities, White ones at that, including Governor Rockefeller and Mayor Lindsay. The rank and file were fairly laid back out on the streets. It wasn't anything like the festive, music-heavy New Orleans sendoff that Armstrong envisioned for himself. The most interesting aspect of the funeral was that the sanitation department showed up the night before to give the adjacent house a facelift in case the cameras panned in that direction.

On another front, I shed worries about the draft. I had never been sure how I would respond to a greeting from Uncle Sam delivered in a big brown envelope. However, I didn't see my reporting for duty, even with the impending drawdown of U.S. troops and the reality that the Vietnam conflict would transform into primarily a proxy war for the U.S. The men born in 1952 were the last class of draftees, but we could still be chosen in the lottery for that class. The procedure assigned a number to each date of the year. Those born on a specific date received the number assigned to that date. Men with a number of 95 or lower had to report for possible induction. Maybe as a college student I had a chance to obtain a deferment. I preferred a definite no, so I needed my birthday to bring me luck. When the lottery was held on August 5, I drew number 359. A resurrected Ho Chi Minh would have to storm down Northern Boulevard for me to be called up.

By this time, I had met Hubert Hammond and Ramón Jiménez, two more mentors. They were among a group trying to establish a nonprofit alternative school, simply called the Community School, and were operating out of a storefront a block from the library. Beginning with the premise that African Americans had the highest dropout rate in the public school system because of irrelevant subject matter, uncaring teachers, large impersonal institutions, and the stifling of Black creativity, they proposed to help people attain high school diplomas, prepare high school graduates for college, and provide instruction to college majors. They encouraged a philosophy of "If you know, teach; if you don't, learn."

Although Marxist-oriented, or at least labor-oriented, Hubert and Ramón were never dogmatic. Hubert had attended Bowdoin College up in Maine. He envisioned an important role for politically sophisticated Black literature. He wasn't impressed with the cultural-nationalist poets I read. He advised me to keep studying Richard Wright. I had already read Wright's poems "Between the World and Me," his powerful description of lynching and its traumatizing effects, and "I Have Seen Black Hands," a vision of millions and millions of Black hands, betrayed by capitalism, joined in revolt with White workers. Wright's mesmerizing word power always provided sufficient reason to read him, but I understood Hubert better when I encountered "Blueprint for Negro Writing," Wright's call for Black writers to mine Black folklore and everyday speech to generate Marxist-informed texts and values, for example, Boris Max's summation explaining the social formation of Bigger Thomas in *Native Son*, and the courageous mother who protected Communist Party organizers in "Bright and Morning Star." The latter character sparked a haiku: *motherly bullets / aimed at the oppressor's heart / always Sue's my girl*.

Ramón, who grew up down the block from Malcolm X's home, graduated from St. John's University and was headed to Harvard Law School. He gave me a copy of Paulo Freire's *Pedagogy of the Oppressed*, newly published in English and destined to become a classic. Freire criticized the traditional role of teachers as the possessors of knowledge to be dispensed to students. He favored a co-intentional model to cure "narration sickness." I would keep in mind, following Freire and Ramón, the need for active student participation in schools as preparation for active, participatory citizenship.

Ramón kept adding to my list. He introduced me to the legendary 8th Street Bookshop in Greenwich Village. At least once a week, we drove in from Queens in his blue Volkswagen Beetle. He headed toward social science and philosophy titles; I took suggestions but mostly sought poetry. Ramón respected poetry. He took my poems, changed all the African American references to Puerto Rican ones, and read his versions to audiences in the Bronx. Then he laughed and told everyone who would listen that he was my poetry instructor and that I had a strange habit of ripping off his poems.

That wasn't the debt I owed. Because he worked in an educational program in Harlem with Karen Troupe, he secured me the opportunity to visit her husband, Quincy Troupe, in their home in Park West Village. Ramón drove me in the Beetle. Quincy asked me what music I wanted him to play. He had what seemed like hundreds of albums, all stacked neatly on shelves, the kind you made with cinder blocks and wooden slats. Thinking of his "Ode to John Coltrane," which I loved, the hippest music I thought to request was Trane's.

Quincy mostly talked about the importance of practice and pursuing the craft. He said political work was necessary but cautioned me about choosing the right running partners. They had to truly have your interests at heart. We talked about poets we liked. He recommended Amus Mor out of Chicago. Eventually, he posed the crucial question, asking me if I had read Pablo Neruda. I had absolutely no idea about any Pablo Neruda. So that was the latest homework assignment.

Latin American surrealism exploded off the page: "A river that the feathers of burning eagles are covering." I couldn't imagine surpassing that imagery. The first book I read (done by Robert Bly) also contained translations of César Vallejo's verse, which was powerful as well. I rapidly collected more titles: Neruda's *Residence on Earth*, *The Captain's Verses*, *The Heights of Macchu Picchu*, *Twenty Love Songs and a Song of Despair*, *Five Decades: Poems, 1925–1970*, and *Fully Empowered*, along with Vallejo's *Spain, Take This Cup from Me*.

Nobody on the street believed that George Jackson hid a nine-millimeter handgun in his hair or a wig to start a rebellion at San Quentin. We knew we didn't have the whole story but refused to trust the official version. Jackson, given the popularity of his *Soledad Brother*, had been central to the rising tide of political consciousness nationwide, especially among inmates, who had been requesting and then demanding improvements in prison conditions. They wanted more favorable work arrangements, enhanced medical care, reduction in exorbitant commissary prices, and adequate representation at parole hearings. However, instead of improving, prisons generally became more repressive. It was no surprise that, less than three weeks after Jackson's death, Attica erupted into the most famous prison uprising in American history, the fuse lit when Leroy Dewer resisted discipline, was sent to the box, and was rumored to be seriously hurt or dead. Governor Nelson Rockefeller, whom I saw being cheered at the Armstrong funeral, refused to visit the prison yet ordered that the facility be retaken from inmate control by force. This resulted in a rampage by law enforcement officers during which dozens of inmates were killed and many others wounded. A state commission reported, "With the exception of the Indian massacre of the late 19th century, the state police assault which ended the four-day prison uprising was the bloodiest one-day encounter between Americans since the Civil War." We knew Attica better than we knew San Quentin in the sense that some of our friends were there. In fact, we knew Dewer, known in Corona as Jacquin (pronounced Wah-Keen), who lived two blocks from me. In fact, his sister Lorraine went to Queensborough with me. We knew Jacquin once had a paper route, worked in the butcher shop, and had just turned twenty-three years old. We also knew that any time he had to do subsequently in New York State was going to be almost unbearably hard.

With all that going on, including the presence at Attica of well-known activist-lawyer (and also poet) William Kunstler, and under the direct influence of Ramón, I thought of becoming an attorney. I would have been too impatient for trial work. It would have been difficult to accept being overruled when I knew my objection was logical. However, I could imagine myself on a team of lawyers working to obtain fair trials, reverse unjust convictions, and advocate for prisoners' education and rights. Even most guilty inmates were going to hit the streets one day, and it was important to consider which version of them you wanted to encounter.

When Ramón went to Harvard, I visited a couple of times, wandering the halls while he was in class. Once I went with Sonny Bargeron, a mutual friend, who drove an orange Karmann Ghia that he didn't like going below eighty. It's the fastest I've traveled from New York to Boston by land. We accompanied Ramón to a protest rally, mainly against the war, on Boston Common. This was part of a nationwide activity organized by the National Peace Action Coalition. An invited speaker, Ramón had to climb onto a high platform and, in the style of the day, he asked Sonny Bargeron and me to go up and stand behind him. I was more interested in my conversation at the base of the stairs with Dr. Daniel Ellsberg of the Pentagon Papers case. He was scheduled to speak after Ramón. A former RAND analyst and a researcher at MIT, Ellsberg released to the press top-secret documents that revealed lies told by the Johnson administration to Congress and the public about the scope and conduct of the war. After surrendering to federal authorities, he faced charges of theft, conspiracy, and espionage. I asked him how he planned to beat the rap. But we didn't get too far because Ramón hurried me up to the platform for his speech. He affirmed antiwar efforts but expressed no love for White leftists who were silent on other issues involving people of color. Somebody threw a whiskey bottle that burst at the foot of the stage, and I told Ramón it was time to speed away from drunken liberals. But he wouldn't shorten his speech. He didn't care what the mood of the crowd turned out to be. He told his truth, unflappable as we knew him to be.

I managed to keep Queensborough classwork under control and in addition became a writing tutor, working in one of the temporary cabins by the front gate. The students I saw, mostly African American, produced writing that exhibited enough lack of awareness of Standardized English to get them into remedial classes and then referred to me. Although from Freire I did grasp the concept of writing as socially situated and political, I had no working theory, either cognitive or social, about their "errors." I fixed them, as they requested, the best way I knew how and explained the rules they had broken. This predated the "Students' Right to Their Own Language" resolution and all the attention devoted to discussing the plight of the Black Ebonics-speaking subject.

I kept up with affairs at the Langston Hughes. Some days I sat at a table chatting with the distinguished artist, illustrator, and writer Elton Fax, who served in residence. A quiet, grandfatherly presence who liked what young writers produced while urging us to take our time to master craft, he was the first writer I knew who had published major books. His *Seventeen Black Artists* served as my introduction to Elizabeth Catlett, Charles White, Romare Bearden, Jacob Lawrence, Faith Ringgold, and a dozen others. In *Contemporary Black Leaders*, Fax rejected the militant-moderate divide and stressed common ground. I was confused by the inclusion of Malcolm X, who had been dead for five years by the time of the book's publication. I didn't question Fax, however. I flipped through the profiles, focusing on Malcolm, Coretta Scott King, Fannie Lou Hamer, Charles Evers, and Ruby Dee. Of Fax's books, the most inspiring to me was his *West Africa Vignettes*, the comments and drawings based on his time in Nigeria, Ghana, Liberia, and Guinea. It made me think more consciously about time and place. As a result, I sketched a four-thousand-word historical overview of the neighborhood, given that I wasn't going to Africa anytime soon.

During my research, I learned about the intriguing Jerry Hunter incident. The sixty-two-year-old Hunter, one of the few African Americans in the area back then, served as caretaker of the Strong Place, located near the Bay. On Labor Day, 1902, Hunter, known to have a short temper, warned a young White man named Thorpe not to trespass on the property. What happened next is in dispute. The official version is that when Thorpe ignored Hunter, Hunter hit him with buckshot. We do know that, for whatever reason, Hunter did shoot Thorpe and the wounded man made it to the police station, prompting an officer named McKenna to try to arrest Hunter. McKenna was also shot and eventually lost an eye. Hunter then holed up and, with his much younger wife, Harriet, held off more than one hundred police officers and vigilantes over the course of seven hours. The couple wounded eight policemen and nine civilians. Finally, as talk of lynching circulated among the crowd, police and bystanders used gasoline to set the house on fire. When Harriet ran out the back door, she was shot by police in the shoulder and captured. Jerry took off for a cornfield, where he was shot in the eye and scalp before being subdued. He wasn't lynched. Instead, he spent three years in Sing Sing. I tried to write a play about the episode. I wanted the action inside of the house to be set in the present while it remained 1902 on the outside. But I could never write plays. A very rough draft was as far as I got.

On the other hand, I collaborated with three other members of the poetry workshop, Randy Latimer, Eric Rawlins, and Lorraine Taylor, to self-publish a small collection we titled *White Paper, Black Poem: A Black*

Tornado. The pages turned out to be blue. Ahmasi suggested that I spell my name "Kiidh" because it was a Swahili way of representing the sound. The name did identity work for a couple of years and is the moniker, no surname attached, used in the chapbook. My lines are agitprop material I needed to write at nineteen. I had to mourn for drug addicts, lambaste hustlers, and call for Black unity and Black militance: *rises an army of arethas / singing "respect" with rifles on their backs*. I have come a long way since, but it's not as though that type of work is behind me entirely.

17

Although my school reading list wasn't nearly as provocative as the one that I pursued beyond the college curriculum, plenty remained to debate in class. I didn't have to wait for reader-response theorists to know it's okay to stretch out on a text. I may have stretched too much at times, but I was never timid. After reading the "The Rockpile," for example, a short story by James Baldwin that sort of ends up in the air, I wrote a paper in which I contended that the boy (John) dies at the end, or at least gets hurt badly. This analysis failed to persuade my instructor, Professor Gillespie, but I insisted that the symbolism and internal logic of the story supported the case I made. We agreed cordially to disagree.

I wrote in the same course, Black Literature in America I, about the humor in two of the Simple stories by Langston Hughes, "Feet Live Their Own Life" and "Promulgations," as well as about the distinctiveness of Black literature in general. I quoted Gwendolyn Brooks, who wrote in her foreword to Lee's *Don't Cry, Scream!*, "If you go into a restaurant desiring tomato juice you do not order the waiter to bring you 'juice': you request, distinctly, TOMATO juice. The juice from cranberries is called cranberry juice. The juice from oranges is called orange juice. The poetry from black poets is black poetry. Inside it are different nuances AND outrightnesses." In a different paper, I addressed existential aspects of Richard Wright's *Black Boy* and how *Native Son* caused the Left to criticize him for lack of proletarian consciousness. I compared Wright's capacity for creative thinking to that of Malcolm X and John Coltrane, and I closed the paper by including Marvin X's poem "Bigger Thomas Lives!"

I saved my disappointment with my hero Hughes for another course. In his essay "Writers: Black and White," he advised, "Be a writer first. Like an egg, then Easter egg, the color applied." He urged Black writers to step outside themselves and see with White eyes. This was opposite Brooks and opposite how I saw the matter of universalism. I wrote that you step inside, like Cervantes, Dante, and Shakespeare, not outside. Our eyes are the only ones we have. We can imagine having so-called White eyes. I suppose that could be what Hughes suggested. Use imagination and employ perspective. But that seemed a funny—not Simple funny—way to put it.

I enrolled in a poetry workshop with an instructor whose sense of development and aesthetics differed drastically from mine. He called us beginners. To me, that meant someone in the fifth grade. In his view, we might, if we were good enough, become promising poets in our twenties, and mature poets in due time. These ideas aligned with Elton Fax's view, and the instructor would sound perfectly reasonable to me today. But back then, there seemed to be all kinds of outstanding and mature poets in their twenties, including most of the ones I mentioned earlier. The instructor either did not know about them or didn't care. He trumpeted the Euro-style masters exclusively, actions that led me to drop the course.

Oddly, I considered dropping Black American History and probably would have if my homegirl Gerianne Scott from East Elmhurst and this brother from Long Island named Phil hadn't been in the class. If we challenged our African American instructor about some of the content he taught, he always swung the conversation to how disrespectful young Blacks were compared to older Blacks like him. Furthermore, he argued that Black people in the ghetto deface and destroy the very places where they live and thus should stop bellyaching about what government should provide. Phil stayed the most agitated and got bounced from a few sessions under threat of having security guards summoned. He did more ideological scuffling than prescribed coursework. Given our instructor's approach, he had no chance to teach Phil effectively.

As part of my student role, I disc jockeyed one semester. It was almost by accident. When Maurice Ford, Eddie Brown, and I were in the cafeteria listening to the music piped in from the campus station, we started grumbling about the fact that the station hardly played Black music, which was not surprising because the station had no Black disc jockeys. We decided to go to the station and protest loudly. It turned out to be the quickest, quietest, and most immediately successful protest in history. To our amazement, the station manager welcomed us enthusiastically and offered us time slots. Eddie and I accepted. I always opened with Isaac Hayes's "Café Regios" from the *Shaft* album and followed mostly with contemporary jazz from CTI and the new Kudu label, as well as less well-known releases such as Alice Coltrane's "Stopover Bombay" from *Journey in Satchidananda*. Of course, I'd get around to John Coltrane's "My Favorite Things" along with a message for folks to go to class. I was on board with all kinds of events at Queensborough: poetry readings, dance recitals, a live performance by the Billy Harper Quintet, a lecture by Dick Gregory, basketball intramurals. I even posed nude for this sister who was a sculpture student. But I never could get with playing spades in the student lounge all day.

The "music," as we occasionally referred to jazz, became increasingly important, especially live shows. Celebrating my twentieth birthday, I saw Keith Jarrett, just coming off his run with Miles Davis, at Slug's on the Lower East Side. I caught Betty Carter at the Village Vanguard. The biggest event was the CTI concert at the Felt Forum, now named the Theater at Madison Square Garden. The show was on the same Friday night the Jackson Five played the main arena. I rode over on the subway with Pat and Frances—you know where they were headed—and met up with Maurice outside the Forum. We blended into an audience carrying wine pouches slung over their shoulders and waiting for the right moment to light up. A formidable lineup graced the stage, including Freddie Hubbard, Stanley Turrentine, Hubert Laws, Hank Crawford, Deodato, Esther Phillips, Johnny Hammond, Joe Farrell, Ron Carter, and Grover Washington. After the show, Washington, dressed sharply as he was on the cover of his album *Inner City Blues*, stood on the corner smoking a cigarette. We acknowledged him, and he asked how the concert, which was superb, was for us. He seemed to really care about our opinions.

The next month I headed for court. Solitaire's case from the Boulevard incident remained unresolved after five years. He had been convicted of disorderly conduct, filed a successful appeal, and faced retrial while being held on other charges. Rámon worked on the case with the attorney of record, the estimable Eleanor Piel. She convinced me to testify; Ramón made me a research assistant. One issue in the case revolved around whether double jeopardy applied. Rámon planted me in a midtown Manhattan law library for several days to research legal decisions concerning *res judicata*. I'll never forget the phrase. The funny thing is that I'm not sure I ever testified. I found a court document indicating that I testified along with Annette Spencer. A different court document explains that Annette and I were denied the chance to testify because the judge ruled that any testimony that we offered would be irrelevant at that point. All I know for certain is that I was in court and that Solitaire's conviction was upheld. I'm also certain that around that time I lost interest in being even a behind-the-scenes lawyer.

By then I had started working with the Friends of Walter Lee McGhee Committee. While visiting Massachusetts, I met Andrew Vachss, who became yet another mentor. A New Yorker who would soon return to the city, he lived in a house in Somerville, where Ramón and I stayed over one night. He directed a juvenile facility and already, before age thirty, had been a public health worker, a community organizer in several states and in Africa during the Nigerian Civil War, a criminologist, a novelist, and a law student. He was keenly interested in parole systems and working for just outcomes, which meant he argued for the release of convicts given suitable evaluation and stipulations. Moreover, parole could serve as post-conviction relief for those unjustly imprisoned, a fate more likely to happen to the poor and minoritized. It wasn't the cause to pursue in Nixon's law-and-order America if popular support were a goal. That never bothered Andrew.

Through Andrew and Ramón, Walter Lee McGhee, who had been in Trenton State Prison for nine years after a 1962 murder charge to which he pleaded *non vult* to avoid the death penalty, contacted me. It was a simple addition to my correspondence. By then I was running my own literacy campaign—sent poems, received poems, wrote evaluations of creative work, responded to political analyses, relayed information to and from mutual acquaintances, furnished books. McGhee—or Mack, as he called himself—hailed from Chicago Heights. I don't recall how he ended up in New Jersey. Besides expanding his circle of friends, Mack sought to improve himself through taking college courses and to receive feedback on his literary output. After I visited him with Andrew—the first of many trips for me to prisons in New Jersey—he said he was impressed that, unlike most others he met, I didn't run off at the mouth trying to prove I was together. He didn't care much for what he called the "pen and lip kind of revolution." He encouraged me to keep working in the community in ways I saw fit.

Mack wasn't much of a poet; however, the five-hundred-page novel manuscript he sent me to review proved fascinating. While I had been unable to sustain my fledgling attempts at fiction, he didn't have that problem. But Andrew joked that if the parole board read the manuscript, they would never release him. He did fictionalize the crime that landed him in prison. It became a stickup of a club where Ray Charles was performing that went awry, rather than a seventy-dollar gas station holdup. At any rate, he wouldn't match the commercial success of Nathan Heard's *Howard Street*, written while the author was serving time in New Jersey for armed robbery.

Robert Lewis, through Mack, became the next link in my Jersey connection. Lewis had been unjustly convicted in 1964 of the rape of a White woman that occurred the year before when he was eighteen years old. We hear the word "unjust" enough to become jaded. In Robert's case, the victim of the rape testified that he did not do it. Moreover, the prosecutor agreed that Robert did not commit the rape. He did not have to prove he did. Under New Jersey law in effect at the time, his burden was to persuade the jury that Robert was an accomplice. That was essentially the same as charging him with the rape. Working in the prosecutor's favor was the fact that Robert left the scene—or, more accurately, the first scene, where a fight ensued that Robert tried to stop. The rape occurred when the assailants took the victim to a second location. Robert was in the wind by then and wasn't apprehended until almost ten months later. He was given fifty to fifty-seven years, a longer sentence than any of the seven other defendants received.

By the time Andrew introduced Robert to Ramón and me, he had recently been denied parole after being incarcerated for eight years. He had exhausted his appeals before he met Ramón, who persuaded a professor at Harvard to make Lewis's case a class project. The only relief left for Lewis, who had an exemplary record inside, was an expeditious parole. His early letters to me didn't sound very hopeful: "Look what the damn politicians are telling the public about prison reform and rehabilitation—damn lies that people are gullible enough to accept. The word 'rehabilitation' means one thing to society, and yet another to prison administrators, and from the convicted class we know that the only place rehabilitation is found is in the dictionary. Society nor prison officials have never defined or given the definition of rehabilitation for it is nothing more than a means to have individuals conform to a bullshit system that perpetuates their oppression." I wished legions didn't have to go to prison to discover or articulate analyses of the social structure. But there seemed no way around it. In the meantime, folks like Robert would continue to "instruct" people like me: "You must know America, progenitor of violence, has been capable of sustaining the most vicious of judicial and political racism which has subjugated and divided people of color."

My old friends also fancied themselves my teachers. I didn't need Fanon; I had Blue. Still a teenager, his good fortune didn't last too long after he chose the right exit that Sunday morning at 127. *i feel i can be capable of strugle / too / so far i haven't did so good / but now i'm moving / and your acheevements help me along. . . . so write back / i want to keep / intouch / remember / make sure you write.* He was beginning a stretch for bank robbery and began preaching to me about political education and political awareness. Explaining how we end up in places like federal penitentiaries studying for a GED, he insisted, "You have to break down the whole political structure of the world. You know what I'm talking about, too. If you don't, I'll break it down next letter." Over the course of our correspondence that year, Blue pointed to shortcomings of Black militance and Black nationalism: "It's time to move on to a greater task and that is to liberate the oppressed people of the world." He addressed the Panther divide, providing what he claimed was the prevailing perspective of the brothers he talked to inside who cared about the situation. He explained that both sides were going into the struggle half ready. He supported the West Coast emphasis on survival programs such as free breakfast and the focus on raising consciousness, which was necessary, Blue argued, to imagine beyond God or Black capitalism. The East had the international perspective and wanted to cut off the monster's head, thus supporting armed struggle. But that, according to Blue, would prove too limiting: "It's not going to be on rooftops and that's all."

On the second anniversary of Jonathan Jackson's death, Blue wrote, "I don't think of it as dying because through his actions he brought about a flash of light in many Blacks' minds." He also addressed a serious matter, the fact that I didn't totally embrace Marxism. He responded, "I think you should read what I have to say in the following pages carefully. And it might help you a lot." He commenced by asking, "How is it possible to justify the criticism of a political viewpoint that bases its principles not on an abstract dogma but on a systematic analysis of objective reality?" Then he proceeded to extol the value of "scientific ideology," the various revolutionary elements—sometimes proletariat, sometimes peasants—relevant to China, Vietnam, Mozambique, and the United States. Blue could always rap. For him, it used to be the doctrine of the Five Percenters, or the Nation of Gods and Earths, though I think they called the women moons back in the day, at least in parts of Corona. Now he was improving as a writer. He generally asked about my sisters and told me to keep trying to help Solitaire, with whom he had crossed paths in the federal detention center on West Street. People talk, Blue said, but few show up. I hoped he eventually would.

Manuel vied for the position of my primary teacher. It never dawned on him or Blue that I did okay when I *didn't* listen to them. He greeted me, his "beloved brother," in the "Arabic greetings and National greetings of Peace and Paradise: As Salaam Alaikum." He called me his "street friend" whom he now realized was his "brother in every sense of the word." To him, the realization came with responsibility: he had to look out for my well-being. Based on his investigations, the only man totally with Black people, a man outstanding in all fields, was the Honorable Elijah Muhammad. He told me to read Muhammad's *Message to the Blackman in America*, which I had already read, and in one letter he copied in print the entire foreword to *This Is the One*, by Bernard Cushmeer (Jabril Muhammad). He instructed me to attend the Temple on Northern Boulevard at 105th Street on any Wednesday or Friday night at eight o'clock. The Temple was one block from his home. He had passed it a million times.

Anyway, I had already visited the Temple and heard a lecture about the cycles of history. Timothy 5X and Benjamin 23X, brothers on my shift at the airport, had persuaded me to go. But I was looking for information, not conversion. I could have been properly termed an agnostic theist who embraced the best of Christian culture. I could accept the fact of a Creator. Harder to accept was that a Creator ran everything in Corona. In 1972 drugs were still more flow than ebb. The grip of the streets—the hand and the hand behind the hand—remained strong. Within any two-block radius in central Corona, you likely could identify twenty absences, that is, folks away in prison.

For my fourth and final semester at Queensborough, Billy Croker, three years older than I, served as my primary mentor on campus. I ended up as the best man at his wedding. From 107th Street, Louis Armstrong's block, and then living in Lefrak City, which they now call Corona but we didn't, Billy had tuned out formal education then tuned back in time to become a very successful student. He was among the first wave to enroll in the City University of New York Baccalaureate Program, an interdisciplinary, intercampus program in which, under the supervision of a faculty adviser, you designed your own degree and could receive life-experience credits. One day, while we were driving around in his cream-colored Nova, Billy told me that the program would suit me ideally and later walked me through the admissions process. In January 1973, with good grades to spare, I transferred to Queens College, a four-year institution to which I probably would not have been admitted two years earlier. Having completed eighteen courses, six in English, I had mainly sampled, unconcerned with the specific requirements for the AA degree. With the life-experience credits I received for various writing projects, I was slightly more than halfway to a BA.

I returned to campus in June to receive an award from the English department, a second-place recognition for creative writing. First place went to Chuck Wachtel, a person I had sat in class with and respected a great deal. I remember, or think I do, his writing a poem about an Edward Hopper painting. Something like that. In any case, his poetry and fiction career shows that the faculty at Queensborough knew what they saw. Check him out.

18

I needed my sports. Although I played in a few tournaments, basketball teams could be cliquish and disorganized. It never seemed easy in my circles to assemble a whole semi-pro football team for regular practices. After being invited, I went to Astoria Park to join a squad only to be restricted to drills because not enough players were on hand for a scrimmage. Boxing became the challenge. Bernard Roberts won two state heavyweight championships while away at college in New Mexico and lost to fierce bomber Earnie Shavers, certainly no disgrace, at the 1969 National Golden Gloves in Kansas City. Back in the neighborhood, he joined the school project. We talked boxing while he showed me a few things about balance, footwork, and movement. He knew the legendary Sandy Saddler, two-time world featherweight champion, who trained fighters at the Maritime Union gym on 17th Street and 9th Avenue. While I was winding down at Queensborough, the gym became my hangout four or five afternoons every week. It wasn't the wisest choice for a twenty-year-old to try to mix it up with sparring partners who had been receiving formal instruction for years, but it was fun for a while. Sandy, for example, was a great personality. Dapper with a little bop in his stride, he called me Schoolboy and told stories about his travels around the world—Mexico, Panama, Canada, Cuba, Chile, Argentina, Venezuela, France, Japan, the Philippines—asserting that he had never seen racism worse than that in the United States. Concerning the sweet science, he said I was starting with impressive athleticism and a good jab. I wasn't really trying to "start." Guys had been training since they were nine or ten. I had nerve, though, or maybe I was testing my nerve. In the back of my mind, I knew I wasn't the most confident person concerning confrontations.

There was no better test than Nelson LaSalle from Puerto Rico. He was on the verge of turning pro at light heavyweight, my weight class, and over the next two years would rack up eleven professional wins, including five knockouts. Naturally, I took almost daily drubbings. One day I nailed Nelson with a right hand, and he was ecstatic. "Sí. Sí." He wanted me to learn. However, the wish didn't supersede his own interests. He was not letting up. An older guy who worked out at the gym hitting the heavy bag and speed bag approached me in the locker room to advise me to stop sparring with Nelson. He stated that I had talent but was going to be quickly ruined if Sandy kept me in over my head. I'm sure he was correct if the issue were long-term development. That wasn't my game. I kept sparring with Nelson.

Fortunately, I had less painful times. Tony Perez, who refereed Muhammad Ali's comeback fight against Jerry Quarry and would work Ali-Frazier II, dropped by the gym for a workout. Nelson wasn't around, so Sandy asked Perez to give me a few rounds. I was puzzled that Sandy wanted me to spar with this slightly built forty-year-old man—more puzzled when I couldn't lay a glove on him. Perez had been an excellent amateur in the army and still had moves enough for me. He slipped punches, rolled along the ropes, spun me, danced away. The only saving grace was that, unlike Nelson, he didn't have the power to punish. Sparring with Perez was like trying to swat an annoying fly.

Surprisingly, I discovered at Maritime that boxing is a team sport. Sparring should be mutually beneficial when possible. Several of my gym mates became upset when I pounded an out-of-shape heavyweight who returned to the gym after a layoff. I should have been helping him ease back into a routine but didn't understand that because I thought about all the blows I had taken. The heavyweight wasn't upset, however. He simply warned me that I wouldn't always catch him slipping. On another occasion, a brother named Duke, a welterweight I sparred with, informed me that we would take it easy because he had been out partying the night before. I heard this as an opportunity to press him relentlessly and spark him up. The next day he didn't say a word. In the ring, he hit me with one blow so hard I saw stars. Yes, I can attest that the phenomenon is real and hurts like hell. With ten-ounce gloves, instead of the sixteen-ouncers we wore, I would have been knocked out instead of badly stunned. I stumbled, but Duke didn't follow up. He knew I had received the message. He later told me that he was coming off a good night's sleep and had been barely able to wait to get to the gym. He was ready to spar at seven o'clock in the morning.

My favorite aspect of going to Maritime, other than talking with Sandy, was hanging with the Santana brothers, Roberto and Tony. From Bedford-Stuyvesant, they were fascinated with talk about my car, a 1965 El Dorado convertible, sky blue with a white ragtop. Auntie, now married and living in New Rochelle, had a '71 model, and Uncle Jack ordered a '73. That gave me my chance to be a genuine stereotypical Negro, that is, park a Caddy every night in front of a run-down house. Turn it down, though? No way. The Santana brothers not only wanted to see the car, they also wanted to drive it. Because I didn't take the car to the gym, they took the subway with me to Queens just for the opportunity to drive around Corona–East Elmhurst a little until I drove them to Brooklyn.

Although only sixteen, Tony had years of training behind him and entered the Golden Gloves, which he would win twice. With my limited experience, which consisted of sparring and a few exhibitions by then, I entered with him. Sandy couldn't talk me out of it because he hadn't returned in time after his trip to Kingston, Jamaica, where he helped George Foreman prepare for his challenge to Joe Frazier. Instead, Bernard accompanied me to the arena, the same Felt Forum where I saw the CTI and Kudu stars. I drew an opponent from the program at Howard Houses in Brownsville. The rest happened quickly, literally, and seemed unreal. I walked into something during the first minute and went down. I bounced up quickly; the referee, Randy Sandy, asked me if I knew the day and my location. I stated that it was Wednesday at the Felt Forum but didn't say it right, I guess. He stopped the bout. My opponent went on to win the tournament, a young woman celebrated the end of all that training, and, except for a few exhibitions put on by Izzy Zerling, a friend of Sandy, Schoolboy was back in his primary milieu.

CUNY BA students were not required to declare a major. Nonetheless, I decided to fulfill the requirements for a major specified by the English department at Queens. That entailed working through some of the canon and, for my chosen track, taking creative writing classes in poetry and fiction. Because it was the spring semester, I didn't begin the two-semester survey tied to the *Norton Anthology of English Literature*. Instead I enrolled in a course on literature and politics, an obvious choice for me, and an offering on John Milton. Malcolm X read *Paradise Lost* while confined to the Norfolk Prison Colony. He recalled that, in his view, Milton and Elijah Muhammad had the same message: Europeans, following the devil, were against God. I wanted to read the detailed description.

In Literature and Politics, labeled English 64 back then, we read writers such as William Blake, W. B. Yeats, and Herman Melville. Of the three, I preferred Blake's prophetic impulses and his sense that art can have a role to play in revolutionary movements. In a brief written assignment, I pointed, like many, to his poem "London" as a critique of modern capitalism and religion. As for Yeats, I didn't like his art-for-art's sake orientation. I agreed with Meredith Tax's criticism that "Easter, 1916" exhibits bourgeois romanticism. Not having enough information, I didn't go so far as to concur that some of Yeats's poetry represented a betrayal of the Irish Revolution. I slotted Melville, along with his constant grappling with ideas of good and evil, close to Blake. I saw parallels between *Benito Cereno* and the current Black freedom struggle. Babo, the insurrectionist, exhibited, as popular opinion went, both heroism and cruelty. I viewed him more as heroic and would have been able to make a more precise call if Melville, in addition to portraying action, had let him speak. Although I wrote "intelligently," as Professor Kizer remarked, I should have refrained from "shaky generalizations" and instead compared the writers by focusing on specific images and ideas in their respective works. His assessment was fair without a doubt. Unlike how I attended to detail in discussing Baldwin's "The Rockpile," I tended to be polemical in papers for class. I fronted political implications at the expense of building cases from the texts at hand.

I did better with examples by the time of my final assignment, which was on three Claude McKay sonnets, "If We Must Die," "The White House," and "Outcast." However, I received a slightly lower grade. I hadn't cleared the topic with Professor Kizer, a fact that didn't please him. He also didn't care for McKay's work and said he would have suggested "better poets," such as Amiri Baraka and Ishmael Reed. He confessed that he cared little for McKay's work because of the stilted and archaic language, although he conceded to liking "Outcast." And he noted that, in terms of discussion, I did a "fairly good job."

Professor Kizer was pretty serious, but Professor Starkman didn't hardly play at all. An acclaimed scholar, she warned us on the first day that she taught a Milton course at the CUNY Graduate Center and lacked the time to create a separate undergraduate syllabus. You had to roll how the graduate students rolled or find something else to do. One assignment was to defend a book of *Paradise Lost* against published criticism. I chose to defend Book VI, in which the fallen angels are driven from heaven, against Marjorie Nicolson's argument that it was unconvincing and inartistic. By Nicolson's reasoning, angels are indestructible; therefore, no suspense can exist in the narrative of war between armies of angels. A Satan fan, at least in the framework of the poem, I felt with him the force of Abdiel's attack that causes Satan to recoil those ten steps and wind up on bended knee experiencing pain for the first time, writhing to and fro. I also disagreed with Nicolson's contention that *Paradise Lost* is inferior to the *Iliad* and the *Odyssey* because those epics contain the drama of death. To the contrary, I thought Milton created comparable tension by delaying Book VI. After meeting the fallen angels in Books I and II, I became antsy for the details of the battle that drives them from heaven even as I knew the outcome, although I did not know that Michael and Gabriel, despite orders from God, could not prevail until the entrance of the Messiah. I made my points but again didn't illustrate them sufficiently.

I demonstrated more skill regarding *Comus*, the assignment being to address the controversy generated by A. S. P. Woodhouse, who asserted that the masque was much weightier than a simple allegory of the triumph of virtue over vice or soul over flesh. I favored opposing opinions by Sears Jayne, Robert Adams, A. E. Dyson, and John Diekhoff. While I addressed the criticism well, according to Starkman, she noted a technical problem that I would struggle with for several semesters: I confused semicolons with commas. Must have been all those classes I skipped in high school. I often used a semicolon before "and" or "but" in compound and complex sentences. Not until Professor Harriet Zinnes told me she was tired of my semicolons and gave me Xeroxed pages from a usage guide, assuring me that "this is going to be easy for you," did I start punctuating properly 99 percent of the time. Overall, my writing was occasionally wordy— "the marriage situation" instead of simply "marriage"—and overly self-conscious. I was a bit of a neologist, breaking off a word here and there like "denouncement" for "denunciation" and "conciliate" for "reconcile." And I confused "sarcastic" with "satiric." I didn't ace any assignments at Queens that semester and shouldn't have in such a fine department. But I wasn't far off the goal with my basic B+ game and kept putting in the reps.

Not wanting to lose momentum, I tackled the *Norton* that summer under the guidance of Professor Barbara Fass. In a brief paper, I compared the insignia on Beowulf's shield, the boar's head signifying strength and aggression, to the pentangle, symbol of chivalry, holy faith, and truth, on the shield of Sir Gawain. I learned that the themes of the Loathly Lady and of Eve were leitmotifs of the medieval and Renaissance periods, as was the concept of *contemptus mundi*. They spoke to the question of illusion versus reality. We were given an assignment, yielding my first A– at Queens, to compare an unidentified passage of nineteenth-century poetry (later revealed to be an excerpt from John Davidson's "All Hallow's Eve") to Chaucer's "The Wife of Bath's Tale" and Book I of Spenser's *The Faerie Queen*. Indeed, beware of illusions, Mr. Redcrosse Knight! Don't blow it with Una and get played by Fidessa, who actually is Duessa. I think we read *Henry IV, Part I*, although I don't recall writing about it, only being amused by Falstaff.

Leslie Epstein had completed his first novel, *P. D. Kimerakov*, and wouldn't be at Queens for long. It was my good fortune to catch him there. An engaged instructor, he took interest in the fiction experiments of all his students. On reading my sketches of scenes from the neighborhood, he encouraged me to keep writing, citing dialogue as my strength.

I took a poetry writing course with Stephen Stepanchev, whose *Mining the Darkness* was forthcoming. An amiable man of about sixty, he lived near the school and wrote a lot about his neighborhood. He would become the first poet laureate of the borough of Queens. Although Stepanchev exhorted us to live on the frontier of language, he didn't seem too familiar or comfortable with the idea of a Black frontier. The wonderful poet Lorenzo Thomas, whose poetry appeared in *Black Fire*, *New Black Voices*, and *The Poetry of Black America*, had been his student, a fact that became the basis of his main advice to me: just read Lorenzo. *in 1979, chances are few impressed. i sensed him out there on the frontier of language where our professor had said we should live and i knew he bought albums at triboro records like eddie brown and maurice ford had taught me to do and put in his time in also on the F train and probably E train too which is an education not to be ignored. i later liked the bathers. for him. seemed overly concerned with pound and frost.*

As I closed in on graduation, I studied more poets, for example, W. H. Auden and W. B. Yeats (again), under the tutelage of Charles Walcutt. I judged (punctuating much better, by the way) Auden's "Embassy" to be a "critical comment on the pathetic impersonality of modern international politics." I launched into a polemic about class oppression, bourgeois ambassadors, Henry Kissinger, and the American involvement in Vietnam. But I did move beyond and provide precise takes on images and form in the poem.

I treated Yeats kindlier and more gently this time around. In discussing "Lapis Lazuli," the finest of Yeats's later poems, I wrote, "What I particularly enjoy is that it represented for Yeats, a man who experienced great internal ambiguities and emotional conflicts throughout his life, the attainment of a final disposition that allowed his habitually intense and stormy mind to realize a certain sense of calmness and serenity." I remained unsatisfied by Yeats's hierarchy—art above politics—but was objective enough to appreciate the poem and try to explain it stanza by stanza.

In Harriet Zinnes's course, I read the likes of T. S. Eliot and commented on the bleakness of "Gerontion" and "The Waste Land." I wrote that the mood of LeRoi Jones's "Political Poem" and his response to modernity reminded me of Eliot. I also compared Jones's poem with Adrian Mitchell's "To Whom It May Concern" and decided that in a stylistic sense, "Mitchell has made himself more a voice of the people" than the pre-Baraka Jones.

Zinnes, a notable poet whose work I would read after college, was one of my two most encouraging professors at Queens, Leslie Epstein being the other. In her view, one kept writing to learn how to write better. She commented on one of my vocabulary-creative papers, "I like the clarity of your discussion. The occasional lapse in precise diction will disappear as you engage yourself more frequently in critical writing." She bet on it.

My final assignment at Queens College brought me back to the journey initiated by Quincy Troupe. Building on translations of "Bruselas" by Donald Walsh and Robert Bly, I provided my own version of the Neruda poem, a piece that Bly suggested is "weighed down by harshness, despair, loneliness, death, constant anxiety, and loss." I didn't explain my attraction to the poem—that "feathers of burning eagles" line—but covered my pertinent choices, especially when they diverged from Walsh or Bly.

After a late start, I completed college in three and a half years. Because the CUNY BA was still new, no graduation ceremony ensued. In June 1974, I took the subway down to the CUNY Graduate Center on 42nd Street, the administrative home of the program, to pick up my diploma. At that point, pursuing an MA in English wasn't my plan. I thought that would mean reading a lot more Anglo literature, and I didn't want to do that in courses. I had applied to only one graduate program, the University of the Pacific, which advertised an interdisciplinary doctorate in which students could design their curriculum. Students who had earned the bachelor's degree could enroll, so I sketched a course of study involving a heavy dose of African American literature and culture, as well as creative writing. Maybe I could write a play. The school didn't technically reject me; my grades and GRE scores were good enough for admission. The message conveyed was that the program didn't suit my interests. The university returned the money order that covered the application fee.

19

During my last year of college, I held a full-time job. I started with the residential substance abuse program that functioned under the umbrella of Elmcor Youth & Adult Activities, a multiservice organization with multiple locations. We were on Northern Boulevard between 107th Street and 108th Street. Working in my home community was ideal. Under the leadership of Ottley Brownbill, Lou Benson, and Jeff Aubry (future Assemblyman Aubry), we offered legal, counseling, and educational services. I began as a counselor on the second shift. We were responsible for client safety and the security of the building, ensuring that the residents' chores were completed satisfactorily, keeping track of the comings and goings of residents who had passes or court appointments, and writing notes for the next shift of workers. Perhaps most important, I learned how to participate in therapy sessions, although I was only half-hearted about it at first. Thinking every patient was me, I thought political awareness and willpower the sole requirements for conquering addiction. There would be no problems if everyone comprehended one of my favorite essays, Michael Cetewayo Tabor's "Capitalism Plus Dope Equals Genocide." I possessed empathy but not enough sympathy and understanding—or enough reflection on my own struggle—until several colleagues began to complicate my view and make me a better practitioner. In a few months, Lou, our program coordinator and energy center—he called us "my guys"—promoted me to head counselor. Now I led groups and helped to make staffing decisions.

I recall talking a great deal on the second shift with fellow counselors William Dobie and Robert Judd. Dobie was one of the spontaneous poets who showed up at our library events. An engaging speaker, he paid close attention to language use around him. He had a fondness for the phrase "for all intents and purposes," which he picked up from our director Brownbill, who was a sharp rhetorician. Brownbill argued that instead of advocating socialism, activists should say they oppose excess profit in lieu of human need. He figured that phrase would increase their audience although, for all intents and purposes, they were saying the same thing. I think of Brownbill sometimes when I wonder about the work, or maybe damage, done by "neoliberalism," "respectability politics," "toxic masculinity," and "post-humanism." Or what if Black activists had explained positions without relying on "woke"?

At any rate, in terms of oral competence, no one was more engaging than Dobie. I still wonder about his writing ability. During the closing minutes of any shift that we worked together, he found it necessary to do a final check of the house, leaving me in the office to make the entries in the activity log. In the program, we often talked about survival skills. Dobie had some good ones.

Judd was a generation older with a lot of wisdom to go with the age. During slow times, we played chess and talked about all sorts of things, including the arts. A professional actor, he possessed an expressive, modulating voice. But sometimes, after a couple of nips of Scotch, he would lose control, like the time we filmed an amateur boxing show. While I did the blow-by-blow, Judd served as the color commentator. At one point, he became so impressed by a contestant's movement that he burst out, "Look at that muthufucka! Look at them muthufuckin feet! Oooh." Judd might have gone off script, so to speak, but he was perfect as the piano player Toledo in the Broadway production of August Wilson's *Ma Rainey's Black Bottom*.

Playwright Ed Bullins did video work for Elmcor. He didn't shoot the boxing show, but he came around one afternoon to see Brownbill. I had read his *We Righteous Bombers*, published under the name Kingsley Bass Jr. in the anthology he edited titled *New Plays from the Black Theatre*. After a few minutes of small talk—I didn't broach the issue of depicting revolution and revolutionaries—he suggested that we ride around and shoot footage of various scenes. It just so happened that Bobby Seale was scheduled to speak at Queensborough. I suggested we go out there; Ed agreed. We took his Toyota station wagon, in which he had already packed the equipment. As we rode along, I wondered aloud if Seale would mind us showing up out of the blue and filming him. Ed said it was cool because Seale used to be in his drama workshop on the West Coast. I don't recall much else about the event, which was held in the student lounge. I do remember Seale telling the audience that there was no such thing as dropping out of the system. White hippies always spoke of dropping out. Seale advised that instead of dropping out, those same White people should further populate small towns in the South and become voting majorities.

Eventually, I worked on the first shift and on several special projects, including the creation of a 110-page booklet titled *The Louis Armstrong Memorial Project*. Designed to attract funds to establish a cultural arts center in Armstrong's name, the volume, on which I collaborated with Andrew, includes essays describing the neighborhood and presenting the rationale for the center, interviews with staff, reports of Elmcor's positive track record, and letters of support. However, the centerpiece is the fifty-five-page photo poem by Andrew and me titled "A Glimpse about My Place/My Time." Andrew took about eighty-five pictures of the worst sites in the neighborhood—abandoned buildings, dilapidated homes, overgrown vacant lots, piles of discarded junk, litter such as wine bottles in the street, and a craps game in front of a liquor store, among others. We stacked the pictures, and as I worked my way through them, I composed the lines starting with, *welcome to my place / the unwanted destination / ghost town of warped destiny / an infested wasteyard of junk / lined by poverty sidewalks / of dilapidated shanties / and cemetrical structures / joined with glassy tombstones / wrapped in brown paper*. Despite the bleak beginning, the piece ends on an optimistic note after pictures of renovations at Elmcor were added, and I invoked Armstrong's recording "Some Sweet Day."

After the booklet dropped, Brownbill assigned me to our next major fundraising effort, a concert to be staged at the Louis Armstrong Memorial Stadium, which was the old Singer Bowl from the World's Fair. Legendary tap dancer and East Elmhurst resident Honi Coles, who had toured with the bands of Count Basie, Duke Ellington, Cab Calloway, and Billie Holiday, as well as with Armstrong's band, currently worked as a production stage manager at the Apollo. Although he was past sixty, he was still a decade away from his role as Tito Suarez in *Dirty Dancing*. An avid golfer, he had a net backstage for practice and, reasoning that the golf balls don't hit back, invited me to visit him at the theater.

Coles was our key link to the entertainment world. Basically, I shadowed him or chauffeured him around, doing whatever he and Brownbill needed me to do to bring the show together. I drove him several times to the Armstrong residence and joined him for meetings with Lucille Armstrong, whom he knew from his days touring with her husband's band. Although I had been around the Armstrong residence, those were my first trips inside. I marveled at the television placed into a wall recess.

I don't think we hit the financial goals for the concert. Nonetheless, the show was first-rate, featuring Main Ingredient, the Jimmy Castor Bunch, Slappy White, and others. *Afrodisiac* is one of my favorite albums of all time, from the cover onward. In the sweltering heat, Cuba Gooding removed his suit jacket and placed it on the side of the stage while his group performed. He left his sunglasses with the jacket. Someone from Corona, whom I knew, promptly stole both items. Livid when he found out his belongings were missing, Cuba pleaded to me that the thieves be caught and brought to him. I listened and understood the bravado but paid the request no mind. I knew that he did not know what he was asking. Those guys did what they did for fun. They could be much more dangerous.

While doing the promotional work, I pressed forward with Ramón and Andrew on the prison work. Mack neared parole. Robert had received a two-year hit. In the interim, Andrew and Ramón undertook extensive preparations for the next hearing. With their diligence, Lewis had a shot, though probably a slim one. Fortuitously, he received a break a few months before the new hearing when the prison psychiatrist Dr. William King, the major voice responsible for the parole denial, was arrested for conspiring to kill his former wife, her husband, and her sister. King, agitated over his divorce, made enough threats to be committed twice to psychiatric facilities in his home state of Pennsylvania. He managed to have his arrest records expunged. The kicker is that he wasn't even certified as a doctor because he never passed the boards, twice failing the tests administered by the American Board of Psychology and Neurology. At Trenton State Prison, he recruited an inmate to commit a hit for him. However, the inmate strung him along and alerted prison officials. In a scenario worthy of the Investigation Discovery channel, an undercover cop posing as a hitman met with King in a hotel. When officers later stormed his office to arrest him, King reportedly fainted. The scandal made numerous media outlets and probably helped Lewis, given that his case was due to come up again before a hostile King. He was released from prison before the end of the year.

On the outside, Robert became director of the Ad Hoc Parole Committee to address prisoners' primary concern: the need for a consistent and legible parole process. We felt that contract parole would inject objectivity into the process by having the board specify the benchmarks by which an inmate could achieve parole. Andrew returned to Trenton many times to interview three hundred inmates about parole denial to describe a pattern. I often accompanied him. He discovered that the board usually served as judges after the fact of conviction. Violent offenders had already been given longer sentences, so parole hearings should not be re-sentencings. He also found, unsurprisingly, that the board was prejudiced against inmates like Lewis who maintained their innocence. Clearly, the parole system was broken, and officials, made jumpy by a riot at Rahway that occurred two months after Attica, were more receptive than usual to proposals. By spring 1974, Andrew had drafted a new parole act for which we aimed to garner legislative and administrative support. Ann Klein, the commissioner of Institutions and Agencies, invited our input when she convened the Correctional Master Plan Policy Committee. The report eventually released by the committee, titled the *New Jersey Correctional Master Plan*, sampled liberally from material we had submitted. The state would move in the direction of contract parole.

On one trip to Trenton, I requested a meeting with Clark Squire, more widely known now as Sundiata Acoli. A member of the Black Liberation Army, whom I had read about in *Look for Me in the Whirlwind: The Collective Autobiography of the New York 21*, he had been sent to the prison in March 1974 after he was convicted on charges of killing policeman Werner Foerster a year earlier during a shootout on the New Jersey Turnpike. In a separate trial, Assata Shakur was convicted on the same charge. At his sentencing, Sundiata remarked, "The Black Liberation Army has been accused of killing policemen. All we do is stop the police from killing us. If the police don't want to get killed, they should stop murdering Blacks and Third World people." Not eligible for parole until 1993, he was released in 2022 after being held in custody for forty-nine years.

Ironically, state troopers pulled over Andrew, Ramón, and me at virtually the same spot on the New Jersey Turnpike. When the siren came alive, I was leaning against the window, nodding off in the back seat of my own car because, being a night owl, I avoided driving to Trenton in the early morning. Picking up my partners ended my shift. Ramón was at the wheel while he and Andrew were discussing some legal or political point, with me half tuned in. An officer positioned himself at the right rear of the car while a second officer, his hand on his service weapon, approached Ramón, who rolled down the window. The officer leaned over, peered over at Andrew, and asked him if everything was okay. Andrew, remaining calm, assured the officer, which in his subject position he could, that everything was fine. The officer told Ramón to drive safely. That's what Ramón had been trying to do, but it wasn't easy with his complexion and wild hair, my Afro in the back seat, and Andrew's complexion and position on the passenger side right in front of me.

Sundiata and I met in the prison library for about twenty minutes, never mentioning his case directly. He knew about our work at the prison and understood that, though commendable, it wouldn't be personally relevant to him for a long time, if ever. He asked me to see what could be done to help James Monroe, a mentally unstable inmate who had killed a guard at the prison two years earlier. According to Sundiata, the twenty-six-year-old Monroe had since been relentlessly brutalized by guards and was mentally deteriorating more and more after having been transferred to the Vroom Building, a maximum-security wing of Trenton Psychiatric Hospital. Sundiata appeared to be genuinely more worried about Monroe's situation than his own.

Such was not the case with a second BLA member, Kuwasi Balagoon. I'm not sure how we got in touch, most likely through Sundiata. They had been co-defendants in the Panther 21 (or New York 21) trial until authorities separated Kuwasi's case so he could face armed robbery charges in New Jersey, for which he received a sentence of twenty-three to twenty-nine years. Kuwasi escaped in 1973 but was now confined to the Vroom Building. I already knew of him because he published several poems in the anthology *Black Fire*, for which he declined to provide an author biography. He expressed instead that his poetry spoke for him, lines such as "Get out of hand and on america's flabby ass / Get out of hand, wipe away the skid marks of oppression and / degradation / Get matches in hand and get out of hand / Get the abominable snowman off the earth."

Like Sundiata, Kuwasi was included in *Look for Me in the Whirlwind*. It so happened that we had a mutual friend, Ahmad, who lived a few blocks from me. A few years older than I, he knew Kuwasi from time they spent together in the Queens House of Detention. One thing led to another, and we were on the road to visit him.

The hospital sat on the right side of a narrow, winding road across from the Trenton Country Club and Golf Course off to our left. Men were putting on one of the greens as we passed by. As we drove on, it seemed that with the various buildings and lush scenery all about, we had entered an old estate. But the Vroom Building, across from the Raycroft Children's Hospital, screamed prison: barbed-wire fencing around the yard, floodlights on the roof. Although we were both on Kuwasi's approved visitor list, he was permitted only one visitor per day. I settled for a seat on the bench while Ahmad entered the visiting hall to a station where he could look through plexiglass and converse on the phone. Kuwasi did most of the talking while Ahmad nodded in agreement and understanding, occasionally laughing. At one point, I think at Kuwasi's request, he opened his jacket to reveal how much weight he had lost. After about twenty minutes, Ahmad gave a clenched-fist salute and exited the hall smiling. When we were back outside, he disclosed that Kuwasi wanted him to obtain some dynamite and bust him out of prison. That didn't happen.

Kuwasi wasn't in the habit of waiting. He wrote to me, actually a message to be relayed to Ahmad—that's what I guessed—"I won't spend too many words on affection right now as you can well understand that my primary concern is the getting of the show on the road. It's so hard when the ranks are still being depleted by yo-yo heads and the sheet-poisoned. I just hope you are remaining strong and can get around to checking out the tools of the trade for me. . . . So foul a sky cannot clear without a storm." Six years after being the twenty-one-year-old published in *Black Fire*, he had become a confirmed revolutionary, a self-described "New Afrikan Anarchist" and a would-be righteous bomber for real, one committed to waging armed struggle against the racist, capitalist, imperialist state. Kuwasi escaped a second time and, while underground, was allegedly involved in springing Assata Shakur from Clinton Correctional Facility for Women and participating in the Brink's armored truck robbery in Nanuet, New York.

Ahmad lectured me about the many aspects of struggle. My concerns had been about arts, education, rehabilitation, the life of the mind, practical interventions in community issues, and the growing carceral state. He firmly instructed me to keep it strictly that way, an order that lined up with advice from Blue—and advice that Kuwasi himself would have given a decade later when in his late thirties instead of late twenties. He wrote extensively about organizational structure—forming anarchist collectives that merged to become anarchist federations. He believed that to minimize the risk of infiltration by agents of the state, people performing aboveground work should not be in contact with underground units. He also believed that mass organization and the will of the people should be the primary foci of a revolutionary program. Of course, he viewed the underground as necessary—and he was made for it.

By the opening months of 1975, I had decided to concentrate on creative writing. Andrew squeezed in writing (on the way to thirty-three novels) while on the verge of starting a law practice based in Lower Manhattan. He represented children and adolescents exclusively and became the top child advocate in the nation, as you can partly discern from his lengthy appearance on *The Oprah Winfrey Show* in 1993. Andrew shared with me a draft of *A Bomb Built in Hell*, featuring the scary character Wesley, almost forty years before it was published in 2012. The John Schaffner Literary Agency, Victor Chapin in particular, represented Andrew during the 1970s but could not stave off numerous rejections.

The center at Elmcor for which I co-wrote the proposal was erected and still operates, but the Community School never became fully operational because we couldn't attract public or private funding or generate sufficient community support. I wrote a piece for the newspaper in which I criticized some community residents for echoing chants and slogans without being serious about change. I concluded, "Community schools must be created—with total community involvement. So move to act/ move to execute. Move from the inert humanoid to the revolutionary performer. From the created to the creator." The school housed a couple of service programs for a while, then folded altogether. Ramón settled into the South Bronx and was becoming known as "the people's lawyer," performing as much pro bono work as work for pay. And the *Transition Press* itself had lost steam. The city experienced hard financial times and looked to the federal government for help. In response, President Ford told the city to drop dead. Well, he didn't really say that; the *Daily News* reported it that way. In some areas, the *News* had much lower standards than the *Transition Press*. Restless, I prepared for my next move.

20

Columbia University offered the John Oliver Killens Writing Workshop, which was open to aspiring poets and fiction writers from the community. Beyond its intrinsic value, it served as a possible gateway for admission to the MFA program. I believe Nikki Giovanni and Keorapetse Kgositsile took that path, although I didn't know it at the time. Killens had taught the workshop for six years before departing for a faculty position at Howard University. The university replaced him with George Davis, a graduate of the MFA program and author of the recent novel *Coming Home*, which was his master's thesis. Killens had been his adviser. To peep into Davis's technique, I checked out the novel from the library and devoured it in a few hours. The fast pacing kept me absorbed in the Vietnam-era war story, and I admired how Davis got the various voices right, each distinct.

I went uptown weekly to participate, taking notes, offering what I hoped was constructive criticism to fellow workshop members, and sharing a few unpublished poems and a couple of fiction scenes that I had presented in Leslie Epstein's class at Queens College. Partly on Davis's recommendation, I was admitted to Columbia with a fellowship for the fall 1975 semester. Although I submitted a mixed-genre portfolio, I chose the fiction track because I thought the program could offer me more in that area. I had a handful of poems published by then, the ones in *A Colonized Few*, a few in the *Transition Press*, a couple in the journal *Johari*, one in the anthology *Treehouse*, and the verses in the Armstrong publication. I doubted the program could help me write 1970s Black poetry. *took pains to shrink the sky / took chains to close your eye*. If I had possessed information about Giovanni's and Kgositsile's experiences, I might have thought otherwise about the poetry possibilities at Columbia. Or maybe not, given the mixed outcomes. Giovanni didn't stay long and Kgositsile graduated.

The novelist and poet Richard Elman (not Richard Ellmann, the critic and Joyce biographer) taught my first-year workshop. I think he also had a say in my admission. Known for his trilogy of novels, *The 28th Day of Elul*, *Lilo's Diary*, and *The Reckoning*, he was a progressive and free spirit, having worked as a reporter in Compton, California, documenting racial discrimination, and in Nicaragua covering the Sandinistas. Perhaps he proved too progressive and free for Columbia as he wrote a pro-Allende editorial and published a novelization of *Taxi Driver*, this second action considered too mass market for a Columbia University faculty member. Of course, low brow didn't bother me. Elman's book is the reason I watched the now-iconic movie and caught the classic performance by Robert De Niro. As a poet, Elman had published *The Man Who Ate New York* and gave several readings around Manhattan to which he invited his students. I enjoyed his work and performance. He talked with me sometimes about jazz and advised me to attend a Thelonious Monk concert if the chance arose. He invited novelist Judith Rossner to class. Her *Looking for Mr. Goodbar* was a hot item around New York and easily made my reading list.

Elman seemed to relish teaching. I was especially fortunate to learn from him that year given that he would soon leave the university. He was a perceptive and encouraging reader and offered loads of practical advice. Almost immediately, he stressed the importance of writing scenes because action will carry the narrative along. He instructed us to plunge into the middle and move around from action to action to action. I had been inclined to think in terms of a grand design into which I would make scenarios fit. Elman emphasized the importance of writers reading, recommending early on William Carlos Williams's *White Mule*. I read the novel while trying to focus on the technical aspects of describing scenes. This wasn't the most fluid way to read, and the story became secondary, such as in the chapter titled "Fourth of July Doubleheader," which detailed Giants-Cardinals games at the Polo Grounds. I became bogged down in analyzing the games. Elman also asserted that we could learn a great deal from unsuccessful novels, although he did not specify examples.

Three weeks into the semester, I visited Elman in his office. He spoke again about focusing on scenes and cautioned against sermonizing. I thought he gestured in the direction of "pure art," but he was more sophisticated. He pointed out that preaching could alienate a reader but the same message could be woven into a character or object.

Let the details tell the story, and let the readers *see* the message. He recommended a random selection of Joseph Conrad's prose, the hair-conking scene in *The Autobiography of Malcolm X*, and, given that I was exploring street life in my work, Vern Smith's *The Jones Men* about drug dealers in Detroit. I passed on Conrad for the time being, revisited the suggested pages in the *Autobiography*, and read Smith's novel, both for style and information, trying to discern why Elman liked it. That I knew much about the world of Lennie Jack and Willis McDaniel was a given, although I didn't get to know their characters—or rather, I knew upon meeting them all there was to know. There was almost no interiority. But Smith wrote scenes very well, with good description and detail. Those were the qualities Elman pushed. Perhaps he had the movies in mind as well because the novel seemed perfect, especially in the era of blaxploitation, for film adaptation. If a studio had been interested, *The Jones Men*, with a Curtis Mayfield– or James Brown–level soundtrack, could have been as notable, for better or worse, as *Super Fly* and *Black Caesar*.

Two stickup men from Corona sometimes escorted me to campus. I had moved to neighboring Flushing by then, in the area around Colden Street, where many from Corona moved into apartments. Some days it seemed like Corona East. I chose the basic 1970s young dude's first apartment setup: portable Toshiba television set, Sony stereo component, album covers mounted on the living room walls, mattress on the bedroom floor, books lined up along the bedroom baseboards. I usually stopped through the old neighborhood on the way to class. That's how I encountered my escorts, who were like a lot of older brothers, doing the wrong thing but encouraging me to do the right thing. They invariably wanted to borrow my car, which by then was a '71 green Chevrolet Impala with a white vinyl top. It was much better on gas, which was important preparation for the next oil embargo and lines at gas stations extending several blocks.

I had two conditions for my chaperones: no stickups using my car and meet me at 116th Street and Broadway, the front gate at Columbia, at the exact time I specified. They always complied on both fronts. I never understood why people taking all that quick money didn't invest a little in at least one automobile, but that was the logic. They even suggested that, given that it might benefit them, I should go back to my old dream and study law instead of fooling around in the School of the Arts.

A third man, a former Corona resident just about Lennie Jack's age, twenty-six, tried to recruit me into the heroin business. I bumped into him while walking across 116th Street toward Morningside Park, widely recognized as the border between Morningside Heights and Harlem. He declared that he was glad to see me doing well but that I should become his lieutenant because he trusted me and knew nobody in the streets more solid. He said he could promise me way more money than a university ever could. I knew he could also promise more immorality, political backwardness, and, almost inevitably, more jail. I was in the streets, but the streets weren't in me except in a positive way.

The semester turned surreal—*Jones Men* overtones—when one of my escorts was shot five times while trying to rob a drug dealer. I remember the chaos of the emergency room at Booth Memorial Hospital and leaving to wander the neighborhood as I prayed for him to pull through. Although I am inclined to take all the help I can get, I doubt prayer had anything to do with the fact that he survived. I worked reflections from that night into an evolving manuscript. I retraced my steps several times with pen and notepad in hand to record observations and strive for verisimilitude. The resultant scene appears in my thesis; a revised version shows up decades later in my novella *The Next Great Old-School Conspiracy*.

A definite highlight of the academic year was *Village Voice* critic Andrew Sarris's film course, which met twice weekly. We saw a film during the first session; Sarris showed up at the second session to lecture, lead discussion, and collect assignments. I had no prior knowledge of auteur theory, which he popularized in the United States, or of his prominence as a film critic, rivaled only by the *New Yorker*'s Pauline Kael. Neither did I know about the rival camps, the Sarrisites and the Paulettes. I guess I was a Sarrisite without even knowing it. But I simply wanted to watch classic movies and hear why they were considered so. The lineup included Ernst Lubitsch's *Trouble in Paradise* (marriage is a beautiful mistake), Charlie Chaplin's *Modern Times* (that nose powder no joke), Alfred Hitchcock's *Rebecca* (Mrs. Danvers trippin), John Ford's *The Grapes of Wrath* (Tom Joad will be there), Ingmar Bergman's *Wild Strawberries* (my favorite stylistically), Orson Welles's *Citizen Kane* (all about Rosebud), and Richard Lester's *A Hard Day's Night* (a treasure for an old Beatles fan).

The only academic downside that year was that I caught the flu and missed the wrong session of the translation seminar taught by program director Frank MacShane. A distinguished guest instructor, W. S. Merwin, visited the class in which I was scheduled to present several translations of Neruda. I wouldn't have the greatest attendance at Columbia; things came up here and there that stuck me in Queens. When an illness occurred on top of that on Merwin day, MacShane could only find my absence "disturbing," the word he used in my year-end evaluation. In contrast, he had complimented my work and given me a good grade. He noted that Elman had spoken positively on my behalf.

I had taken an elective course and had to pass an old-school identification exam. The instructor provided excerpts, sometimes as little as one line, and we were tasked with naming the source and providing context. I didn't miss on any, explaining key points of Nikolai Gogol's "The Overcoat"; Fyodor Dostoevsky's "White Nights"; Heinrich von Kleist's *The Marquise of O*; Voltaire's *Candide*, my favorite story of the group; Johann Wolfgang von Goethe's *The Sorrows of Young Werther*, my second favorite; and Gustave Flaubert's "A Simple Heart." I welcomed the journey beyond the British canon.

During the summer session, I took another literature elective and learned that, in my professor's opinion, Jean-Paul Sartre's *Nausea* should be considered the central text in modernist fiction. We were told Sartre's message: man is just ugly. I scribbled in my notebook, "Not us Black folk." I preferred *Man's Fate*, André Malraux's depiction of the 1927 socialist insurrection in Shanghai in which the rebels failed to wrest power from General Chiang Kai-shek and the Kuomintang. Despite defeat, Chen and Kyo go out on their own terms by committing suicide. I didn't need all the rumination about death. I focused on the other, sometimes revolutionary, philosophical expressions. Personal extinction was not the major consequence in the novel. The key was to assert a sense of being. As Andrew often said, you must make a ripple in the pond.

Man's Fate became important to the story I began to shape, titled "If Life Had a Back Door," inspired by a 1968 Motown recording by the Marvelettes titled "Destination: Anywhere," which contained the bluesy lyrics addressed to the ticket seller at the railroad station: "Destination anywhere / East or west, I don't care / You see my baby don't want me more / This old world ain't got no back door." I suppose those words

144

could have been the epigraph, but I chose instead an adage from Malraux's character Old Gisors, Kyo's father and a former professor of sociology at the University of Peking. He is also addicted to opium. Early in the novel, he muses about the hustler Baron de Clappique who, according to Old Gisors, drinks too much: "It's also possible to choose the wrong vice; many men never strike the one that might save them. Too bad, for he was far from being without worth."

That August I attended the Bread Loaf Writers' Conference up in the mountains of Vermont near Middlebury. I didn't enroll to have work evaluated. I would go to workshops and other events for ten days and soak up information. But the main reason I participated was to meet Toni Morrison, who joined the faculty for the first time. She hadn't yet gone through the literary stratosphere but received considerable notice after the publication of *The Bluest Eye* and *Sula*. She proved to be supportive as well as inspirational. She told me and Charles Lynch, a poet from Brooklyn, not to worry so much about publishing opportunities because if we kept working, we would get our chance. As for completing fiction projects, she advised that if we wrote one page per day, we would have 365 pages by the close of a year. Of course, producing one good, *connected* page per day ain't easy. Nonetheless, I understood the mission. Trusting us to be cool, Toni took us into a reception that was supposed to be for faculty only. Mark Strand, who taught at Columbia for a while, May Swenson, William Meredith, and John Irving were among the attendees. Amid the chatter and tinkling of glasses, people looked at us, accompanying Morrison, like we were important.

Morrison made two featured appearances in the Little Theatre. First, she delivered a lecture highlighted by a reading from *Sula*: the chapter "1923," in which Sula stands on the porch and watches her mother, Hannah, burn up in a yard fire. Later in the conference Morrison absolutely mesmerized us by reading excerpts from the manuscript of *Song of Solomon*, newly completed. She shared parts of chapter 1, the explanation of the naming of Macon Dead and Pilate, and Macon's walk along Darling Street past the home of Pilate, Reba, and Hagar. She read from chapter 13 as well, the run-up to Hagar's death and the subsequent funeral. I'm glad I knew that Morrison was exceptional and not the standard. Elman always reminded us that we could learn a great deal from reading poor novels. Chasing Morrison could crush you.

Other than days spent in the Langston Hughes library poetry section, I don't think I had ever had a stretch of ten days as artistically stimulating as those at Bread Loaf. After a few days, the attendance began to dwindle because some didn't observe a seemingly self-evident rule that I learned from Elman, that is, only bring writing you want to work on to a workshop. If you bring material that you consider finished, you are looking for praise, not constructive criticism, and could get your feelings hurt. That was no problem of mine.

I heard some decent work at workshop readings. One memorable piece described a White inmate killing a "nigger" inmate in a Louisiana prison. I thought the author put too much emphasis on the n-word, though the overall descriptive language and dramatic tension were good. Charles and I, the only African American men at Bread Loaf, joked almost daily about getting off the mountain. The mountain, however, was nothing we couldn't manage. I think the same held true for the two African American women, Melinda Kay, daughter of the renowned classical composer Ulysses Kay and a big fan of *The Bluest Eye*, and Kate Rushin. Melinda, bright and exuberant, loved to keep a conversation going. Kate, known more later as Donna Kate Rushin, was less outgoing. I enjoyed talking with her, though. She was sharp and definitely headed for noteworthy achievement in poetry. She had already been affiliated with the arts center in Provincetown.

Kevin, my roommate in Bread Loaf Inn, happened to know two guys from Corona whom I knew very well. He asked me to please not tell them that I saw him. Knowing what they were about, I wondered what he had been about or was avoiding. Protocol dictated that I should not inquire. I didn't even ask from which neighborhood he hailed. Kevin was on a waiter's scholarship; he had to work the dining hall.

Evenings I played volleyball, often on a team opposing Irving's. We won more than we lost. Irving couldn't be too sharp at volleyball. He needed to complete *The World According to Garp*, destined to be a literary sensation. Other social gatherings were up in the Barn. On the way, I would stop at the phone booth to make calls to New York, the stars appearing very bright overhead.

Kevin offered to drive me home, an offer that beat the hell out of a return bus ride. Melinda rode with us as far as Fort Lee, New Jersey.

2I

Paule Marshall taught me, or tried to, my second year. In most matters, she was correct and I was young. Obviously, the author of *Brown Girl, Brownstones* could offer much, especially considering how good the dialogue is in the novel. But back then, I regarded her as inflexible in terms of the styles and content she favored. I think my street stuff and spotty narrative control were too disconcerting for her. I don't recall any advice from her seminars, only directives to revise.

Most memorable were the visitors. I helped to bring in Toni Morrison, who enchanted everyone as I knew she would. In that class she dispensed the words of encouragement that I have often repeated to writers: you should be better than Homer because you get to read Homer and he doesn't get to read you. Our second visitor was James Baldwin. He sat right next to me at the seminar table and talked about writers pushing themselves to work the language. I paid attention but also thought that my chance had come to resolve the issue about "The Rockpile" that had been lingering in my mind since my Queensborough days. When I put the question to Baldwin after class, he didn't recall the story, at least not readily. When I refreshed his memory and pushed the question again, he maintained that I was wrong. In his view, the story does not suggest that John is to be fatally assaulted. So I went back and read "The Rockpile" again. Danger, blood, fear, and death—or musings about danger, blood, fear, and death—on all the opening pages. The figure of the dead boy, Richard; the rockpile suggesting prison; the father's "heavy shoe" as potential weapon. It all seemed like some heavy foreshadowing to me. Then the "fury" and "deep hatred" in the father's face. By then I knew that a parallel scene existed in Baldwin's first novel *Go Tell It on the Mountain* and that in that version John survives to escape to the safety of the church. However, I remained fixated on the text presented to us as a *short story* and made my interpretive leap. I won't say Baldwin read his own story incorrectly, but D. H. Lawrence said that critics have the job of saving tales from the artists who write them.

I read Lawrence's criticism in another literature elective. Beyond thinking about the role of critics, I was intrigued by his discussion of "man alive" in "Why the Novel Matters." Lawrence wrote, "To be alive, to be man alive, to be whole man: that is the point. And at its best, the novel, and the novel supremely, can help you . . . for out of the full play of all things emerges the only thing that is anything, the wholeness of a man, the wholeness of a woman, man alive, and live woman." No, we don't have to bear history like a backpack. No knowledge is superior to immediate sensation or experience. "Over listening" to tradition could lead to stagnation. But Lawrence wasn't dialectical enough for me when he argued that change was not absolute and also wrote, "The whole is a strange assembly of apparently incongruous parts, slipping past one another." In dialectical materialism, the parts are not slipping past one another but instead forming contradictions. And contradictions, as I understood matters, always led to change.

Yet I preferred Lawrence's "man alive" to T. S. Eliot's "man traditional." The idea that "no poet, no artist of any art, has his complete meaning alone" was unobjectionable. I granted Eliot the point. Nor did I have a problem with the suggestion that what is often best in a writer's work reflects that writer's literary ancestry—or with the corresponding idea that the "historical sense," the sense of the "timeless and temporal together," needed to be developed in anyone who aimed to continue as a poet beyond the age of twenty-five (I was twenty-five). On the other hand, I felt that Eliot's notions of "simultaneous existence" and "depersonalization" merely tried to justify the obscure classicism of "The Waste Land." He privileged a European tradition and a European model for a European diaspora. Black writers should sip from that well but not overdo it. I wondered if Eliot would have read and tracked all the footnotes of a lengthy poem steeped in African and African American history and culture.

I found Kenneth Burke's *The Philosophy of Literary Form* to be cumbersome, though not as much as Eliot's prose. I enjoyed his criticism of the "pure art" position in his essay "The Nature of Art under Capitalism." Burke pointed to the relationship between work patterns and ethics, which is most productive, he argued, when work is tied to

148

cooperation and service. For Burke, competitive capitalism destroys the positive aspects of the work-ethics relationship and promotes a state of acceptance, such a situation being reflected in "pure" or "acquiescent" art. Because "'pure' art is safest only when the underlying moral system is sound," Burke called for a "corrective kind of literature."

Sigmund Freud was my main hit-or-miss critic. I dubbed him brilliant-terrible-spectacular. Although not a Freudian, I appreciated any time Freud provided a clear explication in nonspecialized language. So I liked "The Relation of the Poet to Day-Dreaming," the concept of art as a dynamic involving the move from dissatisfaction to fantasy to wish fulfillment, either self-exalting or erotic, and, because of its aesthetic presentation, as a source of enjoyment for readers; "The Moses of Michelangelo," on the significance of details—the right hand, the beard, the tablets, in relation to the whole work—Elman would agree with that; and "The Antithetical Sense of Primal Words," a dialectical conception of language and the effect of the development of language on the development of dreams. On balance, I certainly embraced the art critic in Freud, but he lost me, at least back then, with "The Theme of the Three Caskets," his take on *King Lear*, and "The Acquisition of Power over Fire," with its phallus analyses.

Meanwhile, I neared completion of a draft of "If Life Had a Back Door." It was far from a good one. Only my most favorable critic, my sister Pat, liked it without qualification. At the end of two years in residence, I still needed to complete the thesis and one more three-credit elective. I didn't worry about the course that summer, choosing to focus on the manuscript. I possessed good discipline; it was nothing to spend ten to fifteen hours, with minimal breaks, on my electric typewriter. Despite my ambition and work ethic, I never did get a handle on the story, partly because it was too autobiographical, and I failed to achieve the distance to analyze the central characters well. The two men, Ronald Rivers and Bobby Stone, one a drug user/armed robber and the other a graduate student, shared a friendship and bond that would be almost inexplicable outside of their world. That relationship indeed could be explained. I had no choice but to believe so, given the life I lived. However, I lacked proper perspective. I would respond to most criticism, usually silently, "You don't know how it is." I failed to follow a lesson I learned from Elman. It is never enough that a story is true in an objective sense, as far as we can determine that. What is essential is that the story *rings* true. Not that it can't be fantasy. Most readers can accept any number of actions. But the characters must seem authentic to readers, whether or not the characters are grounded in reality. The issue for me shouldn't have been "You don't know how it is." The germane point was to develop a wide-ranging and compelling textual response to the key question: "How is it?" I hadn't reached that level.

Besides the conceptual problem, my style proved to be too episodic and uneven. I had a clearer sense of writing scenes—one emphasis I did retain from Davis, Elman, and Smith—but didn't craft mature chapters. Even though I read novels, my manuscript was much more screenplay than novel and would, unfortunately, because I became too attached to it for too long, remain so. I even mixed in playwriting style I had seen in Bullins, a vignette of one side of a telephone conversation. At any rate, I eventually received valuable feedback from several sources. Joe McElroy, who was on the faculty at Queens College when I was enrolled and taught part-time at Columbia, had been asked by MacShane to read the manuscript. McElroy surely "knew how it was." Suggesting that the narrative didn't come off as a whole, he discerned that the central character-voice "doesn't serve a coherent narrative purpose." McElroy couldn't identify the "subject of the narrative." He added, "It's not robbery, nor the origins or causes behind it, nor is the central subject anything these people spend their time doing. And so, as the central character-voice expands and settles into the narrative and what seemed at first to be a lurking plot fails to develop, I seek some prevailing motif, some statement, a magnetic center for the character-voice and the life it presents: but amid talk of prison, protest, sex, love, fantasy-projections set against actual events, failures amid exhilarating energy, I don't find that center." On the other hand, McElroy lauded the "wonderful live language both precise and relaxed," some of the scenes that were "sharply and economically done," and the "over-riding voice and idiom and knowledge of the life." MacShane would provide comments similar to McElroy's: elements of a good book were there, but I had not made them cohere. MacShane, as did McElroy, endorsed the language as "convincing and real" and thought the hospital scene represented the standard for which to strive.

Toni Morrison agreed with McElroy and MacShane, though with much briefer commentary after Andrew's agent Victor Chapin sent the manuscript to her at Random House. She wrote that some parts were *"very good"* and some "extremely disappointing." However, she remained open to seeing how the work progressed. Victor, whose evaluation lined up with the others, would inquire if I had worked on the manuscript. He wondered if I was turning the potential he saw into polish. However, opinions and queries didn't matter much to me by that point because I was no longer that invested in the story, figuring that a treatment of mid-1970s post–Black Power stasis would be dated by the time I addressed all the problems in the text satisfactorily. I had begun thinking that generating more than two hundred pages of scenes, several considered good, a couple *very good*, as assessed by none other than Morrison, would have to represent my time in the program. Where I ended the program, that is, with a full draft to work on, would have been a better place to begin.

The manuscript wouldn't be published but portions would. Enough of school for the time being. I'd make the revisions I had the patience and capacity to make, eventually take that last elective, and move on. Other work would arise. Elman always said never to worry about running out of ideas.

Ahmad went into the bank robbery business and had to flee town a step ahead of the FBI. Through a third party, he sent me a letter with the salutation "Habari Gani Ndugu" and proceeded to inform me of "contemporary happenings," which included what he termed a "bit of bad luck": "i fell on a meatball (wrong place at wrong time). i rose the next day with the blessings of ALLAH—own recon, phony name. they took my prints. now i've got to keep on pushing." Ahmad conveyed that he might be getting tired and sometimes entertained the idea of surrendering. To make that decision, however, he wanted more information. If the charges against him were not as serious as he suspected, he would face them. If they were, he would stay on the lam. Next came his ask: "your lawyer friend—any possibility of aid as far as finding out my exact position? check it out for me. will contact you in near future and advise as to my whereabouts. till then, a luta continua." Ahmad instructed me that any message for him could be sent to his wife, at least for the next few weeks, at the address I had. He added a postscript: "other than aforementioned, everything and everyone mellow!"

During that summer of 1977, Leon Jackson grabbed a permanent place on my sofa. We had worked together at Elmcor. In fact, I had been instrumental in his hire because Lou told him to attend my therapy group and told me to see if we could use him. He became one of the best counselors and court liaisons in the organization's history and always kept me upbeat. Still on the staff, his trip to work from neighboring Flushing took a fraction of the time as his former trek from Brownsville. Everybody liked Leon; everyone in our building knew him and his upbeat chatter. No day got him down. No challenge daunted him. He couldn't quite pull off the promised gourmet meal or really fix your television or car, but his failures were entertaining, if expensive. He could have inspired a version of a popular motto: one hundred dollars but two hundred if you tried to fix it yourself. In fact, I lost my Impala because of Leon, even though it wasn't his fault. A motorist fleeing from the police ran a red light and T-boned my car on the passenger side. Luckily, Leon escaped serious injury. I found another Impala that had the right price tag in an aqua color I didn't like and, after delicately dodging Leon's offer to do the job, had it painted black professionally to match the interior.

Before the singing group Tavares popularized the missing-angel trope with their hit song, Leon walked around asking women if they were angels despite me continually telling him it was a corny line and that he needed to improve his rap. He responded that he didn't need any rap. His technique was to beg. Just beg and wear a woman down. Or at least beg politely enough to be accepted as a funny and flattering friend. I could see his point. At one level, everybody begged—it was just that some had more nerve and silk in their game than others.

A blackout hit New York City that summer. President Carter had been talking about energy conservation but didn't envision it happening that way. Unlike in 1965, the looters went wild mainly because the blackout began around nine-thirty on a hot July night after most businesses were closed as opposed to five-thirty on cool early evening in November. In the Bronx, they smashed the windows at Dick Gidron's car dealership, a favored one among hustlers and celebrities, and drove Cadillacs out of the showroom. I heard that a similar thing happened at a moped store a few minutes from me in downtown Flushing.

The only thing left for us to do in Apartment 7V was to throw a party. Call folks together. Gather frozen and refrigerated food from several apartments. Let Leon orchestrate the preparation. Check the batteries in the boom box. A candle or two. Vibrate in the darkness our way.

Gyrate. Bounce. Drink. Joke. Smoke. Signify. Laugh. Rap. Bump. Slide. Grind. Twist. Twirl. Sing. Shout. Sweat. Be the prose if I can find the proper angle and analyze correctly. Be the unavoidable poetry.

I used to stand on the terrace peering down at the sidewalk below feeling lucky to be able to do so. A Black boy on a tricycle sometimes peddled furiously toward the end of the building. That was the boundary stipulated by his mother. Not surprisingly, he tended to ignore it. "Come back here," she shouted after him once and started in his direction. Then she declared with authority: *Hard head make a soft behind.* Soul music wafted from the open windows of an automobile parked at the curb.

About the Author

Keith Gilyard is the Edwin Erle Sparks Professor of English and African American Studies at the Pennsylvania State University and a former president of the National Council of Teachers of English. He has published widely in the topics of language and rhetoric, including *Voices of the Self: A Study of Language Competence*; *Let's Flip the Script: An African American Discourse on Language, Literature, and Learning*; and *Liberation Memories: The Rhetoric and Poetics of John Oliver Killens* (all Wayne State University Press). He is the recipient of two American Book Awards and the Penn State Faculty Scholar Medal for Outstanding Achievement in the Arts and Humanities.